BRITISH AND IRISH
Country Cooking

BRITISH AND IRISH
Country Cooking

Tony Schmaeling

OMEGA BOOKS

ACKNOWLEDGEMENTS

My tour of the United Kingdom was organised with the precision and attention to detail for which the British are justly famous.

Despite the reservations originally expressed by Peter Ffrench-Hodges and Catherine Althouse of the London British Tourist Authority, my mission to collect recipes and photographs for this book was a complete success.

It was owing to Catherine Althouse's great effort, organisational skill and enthusiasm, that I was able to achieve so much in such a short time.

In the Sydney office of the B.T.A., David Morrey-Jones and Pip Stuart set the whole project in motion and I am grateful to them for providing me with additional pictorial material.

Inspired by the idea of a book on British cooking, a host of restaurateurs and hotel owners throughout England, Wales and Scotland co-operated by preparing authentic local dishes for me to photograph and taste. The names of their establishments are gratefully recorded with their recipes. Without their willing and friendly co-operation this book would not have been possible.

The original idea for this series of cookbooks on the food of Europe came from Kevin Weldon, at the time Managing Director of Paul Hamlyns. I thank him and Warwick Jacobson, the company's Publishing Manager for their encouragement and technical support.

I thank Graham Turnbull of Traveland, whose company sponsored my travels through Europe to collect material for this Viva! Holidays cookbook series. His London office gave me valuable assistance.

On my return to Sydney, Gwen Flanders and her daughter Michelle, with great perserverance, deciphered reams of my illegible longhand and typed it into a neat manuscript. My editor, Susan Tomnay showed good humour, patience (of Job), competence and dedication in putting the whole book together.

This edition published 1983 by Omega Books Ltd,
1 West Street, Ware, Hertfordshire, under licence
from the proprietor.

Copyright © RPLA Pty Limited 1982

ISBN 0 907853 02 1

Printed and bound in Hong Kong by South China Printing Co.

CONTENTS

BRITAIN

IRELAND

Orkney Islands

Western Isles

Highland

Grampian

Tayside

Central   Fife

Lothian

Strathclyde

Borders

Dumfries &
Galloway

Northumberland

Tyne and Wear

Cumbria   Durham   Cleveland

North Yorkshire

Donegal   Londonderry

Antrim

Tyrone

Down

Fermanagh

Armagh

Sligo   Leitrim   Monaghan

Mayo   Roscommon   Cavan   Louth

Longford   Meath

West Meath

Galway   Offaly   Dublin

Kildare

Clare   Laoighis   Wicklow

Carlow

Limerick   Tipperary   Kilkenny   Wexford

Kerry   Cork   Waterford

Lancashire   West
Yorkshire   Humberside

Greater   South
Manchester   Yorkshire

Merseyside

Cheshire   Nottinghamshire   Lincolnshire

Clwyd   Derbyshire

Gwynedd   Staffordshire   Norfolk

Salop   Leicestershire

Powys   West   Cambridgeshire
Midlands

Northamptonshire   Suffolk

Hereford and   Warwickshire   Bedfordshire
Worcester

Gloucestershire   Buckinghamshire   Essex

Dyfed   Oxfordshire   Hertfordshire

West Glamorgan   Mid   Gwent   Greater
Glamorgan   London

South Glamorgan   Avon   Berkshire   Kent

Wiltshire   Surrey

Somerset   Hampshire   West
Sussex   East Sussex

Devonshire   Dorset

Cornwall   Isle of Wight

THE COUNTIES OF
BRITAIN & IRELAND

ENGLAND

SCOTLAND

WALES

EIRE

NORTHERN IRELAND

BRITAIN

INTRODUCTION

The collection of British recipes in this book is in no way complete. I am not even sure if it is typical. But it is the result of a genuine attempt to record the sort of food to be found in Britain today.

In my search I was greatly assisted by Catherine Althouse of the British Tourist Authority who mapped out my journey through England, Wales and Scotland which took me to many restaurants where local dishes are prepared.

I have recorded what I have found and what has been offered to me. The recipes are the interpretation of local dishes by the chefs who prepared them and therefore may not necessarily be true and accurate versions. To me, however, this is the essence of good regional cooking: an individual approach to a basic local recipe.

Yet during my travels I found that regional food was not commercially available to the same degree as in the rest of Europe. There are many reasons for this.

In Britain the most drastic change in the eating habits of the people came with the Industrial Revolution in the first half of the 19th century. When huge segments of the rural population shifted to the towns, regional traditions, developed over the centuries, were suddenly, and in many cases, brutally destroyed. Until then the majority of the population was in one way or another connected with the land.

Suddenly being cut off from the roots of their rural existence and losing the sources of their traditional food supplies, the traditional ways of preparing the ingredients were also lost. What replaced their simple but healthy food was a diet unrelated to anything previously experienced, and barely sufficient for survival.

Of course, this is not the complete picture. The Industrial Revolution did result in the emergence of a prosperous middle-class which tried to imitate the customs of established upper classes, which in turn, had adopted many foreign, especially French, traditions.

Eating habits in Britain were further complicated by the availability of foods from the colonies, by wars and the austerity measures they brought, and finally, by the results of the progress in food technology such as preserving and freezing which made food from all over the world available all year. In general terms, the food of Britain today bears little resemblance to the traditions of eating of one or two hundred years ago.

This of course does not mean that regional, traditional cooking has been completely forgotten. It is alive and well and in recent years many cookbooks have been written about it. There is a definite awakening of interest in traditional regional cooking. However, the interest is not yet universal and the prejudice of many years has to be overcome until it again dominates the cooking scene.

The purpose of this book, in addition to being an interesting cookbook is to achieve at least two further goals. The first one is to provide the cooks of Britain with an additional record of their own culinary heritage and to assist in fostering the interest and therefore the acceptance of traditional regional cooking.

The second one is to show visitors to Britain where they can find true regional cooking. Today as in the past, the tourist largely 'travels by his stomach' and the enjoyment of eating the regional food of the country goes hand in hand with the enjoyment of sightseeing.

Britain today provides a great wealth of things to see: the great traditions which have evolved around its monarchy and which manifest themselves in Royal occasions of pomp and circumstance; the museums and art galleries which house the collections brought together over the centuries when Britain enjoyed power and wealth; its architecture and towns which for hundreds of years had an immunity from the destruction of wars, and most of all, its countryside, rich and varied and in many parts, the guardian of old traditions, including that of cooking.

Food resources vary from county to county and this difference has been responsible for the development of regional dishes. In Britain the differences are not as strongly pronounced as in other countries. However, nobody would mistake the cooking of England for that of Scotland or Wales.

Today a culinary journey through the counties of England, Scotland and Wales is still a rewarding challenge which yields to a gourmet unexpected pleasures at the table.

Tony Annannny

All flour is plain (all-purpose) flour unless otherwise specified.

SOUPS

Beautiful soup!
Who cares for fish, game or any other dish?
Who would not give all else for two penny worth only of beautiful soup!
Lewis Carroll

High praise indeed for the humble soup. Soups have always played an important part in human nourishment; everything and anything edible went into their preparation. Thick or thin, made from fish or seafood, meat, poultry, game and vegetables, it was an indicator of social standing and trade. You could tell the soup of a farmer from that of a fisherman, the country man from the town dweller.

The word *soup* or *sop* — derived from the French — described not the liquid, but the bread which was placed in the bowl. Bread soups exist in the cooking traditions of most countries. Indeed, they are among the oldest and most primitive of preparations. While the old Scots White Soup — a smooth creamy soup poured over bread — goes back only to the 16th century, it is, I am certain, a direct descendent of these old bread soups.

Britain has many fine regional fish soups and today when fresh fish and seafood are available in all parts of the country, they are no longer confined to the tables of the fishermen. In London, I have eaten a very tasty cockle soup which originated in Northern Ireland. Oysters, which until a hundred years ago were everyday fare, are today combined with mutton stock to make the luxurious Welsh Gower Oyster Soup.

Hunting has always been a favourite pastime and there are many fine game dishes in this country. The older, tougher birds and beasts finished up in the soup pot. And when the best parts of beef, lamb or mutton were eaten, there were still the bones, the scraps and lesser parts of the animal to be made into soup. So it's not surprising to find a kidney broth, soups using neck of mutton, shin beef, tripe and of course, oxtail, a favourite during the 19th century.

There are some well known regional soups: Leek soup from Wales, Cheshire soup in which local potatoes and Cheshire cheese are used, and of course Scottish Oatmeal soup.

The soups of the British table may not be as famous as some of its neighbours on the Continent but they do represent a tasty offering for any meal.

Watercress Soup

*This recipe comes from the **Bush Hotel** at Farnham in Surrey.*

Serves 4

30 g (1 oz) butter
1 small onion, finely chopped
1 small leek, finely chopped
1 bunch watercress, washed
2½ cups (20 fl oz) chicken or veal stock

250 g (8 oz) potatoes, peeled and sliced
pepper
salt
¼ cup (2 fl oz) cream

1. Melt the butter in a saucepan and sauté the onion and leek in it, without allowing them to brown.
2. Chop the watercress, reserving a few leaves for garnish.
3. Add the chopped watercress to the onion and leek in the pan and cook for a few minutes.
4. Pour in the stock and add the potatoes, salt and pepper.
5. Simmer for 30 minutes.
6. Pass the soup through a coarse strainer, return it to the pan and add the cream.
7. Reheat gently, being careful that it doesn't boil.
8. Pour into warm soup bowls, float the reserved watercress leaves on top and serve.

Right: Carrot Soup (see p. 13), Watercress Soup (see p. 10), Friar's Chicken Soup (see p. 13).

Cawl Cennin a Hufen

Cream of Leek Soup

*From the **King's Head Hotel** at Monmouth in Wales.*
The leek is the national emblem of Wales so it is not surprising that it appears in many fine dishes. Cream of Leek Soup, a refined version of leek and potato soup, does justice to this great vegetable.

Serves 8

625 g (1¼ lb) leeks, washed
60 g (2 oz) butter
375 g (12 oz) celery, chopped
7½ cups (1.75 litres) lamb or chicken
   stock

30 g (1 oz) parsley, finely chopped
salt and pepper
60 g (2 oz) diced cooked chicken
   or lamb (optional)
⅔ cup (5 fl oz) cream
sippets

1. Slice the leeks thinly and reserve some of the green slices for garnish.
2. Melt the butter in a large pan and cook the leeks and celery over gentle heat with the lid on the pan until the leeks are soft but not brown.
3. Add the stock, bring to the boil and simmer for 1 hour, skimming if necessary.
4. Purée the soup in a blender, return it to the pan and add the parsley, reserved leek slices and diced meat. Season with salt and pepper.
5. Add the cream and reheat the soup without allowing it to boil. Serve with sippets.

Pea and Bacon Rib Soup

*From the **Waterside Restaurant** at Romiley, Manchester.*

Serves 8

500 g (1 lb) bacon ribs,
   soaked overnight in water
30 g (1 oz) butter
125 g (4 oz) onions, chopped

125 g (4 oz) carrots, diced
60 g (2 oz) celery, diced
500 g (1 lb) dried split peas
salt and pepper

1. Put the bacon in a large pan and cover with 10 cups (2.5 litres) water. Bring to the boil and simmer for 1 hour.
2. Melt the butter in a pan and cook the onion, carrots and celery for 8 minutes, making sure you don't allow them to brown.
3. Add the peas and cook for a further 2 to 3 minutes, stirring well.
4. Add this to the stock and ribs, season, bring to the boil and simmer for 2 to 3 hours. Skim when necessary.
5. Remove the ribs and put the soup through a blender. Return the soup to the rinsed out pan, add the ribs and reheat.
6. Serve with sippets.

Carrot Soup

Serves 4

375 g (12 oz) carrots, chopped
100 g (3⅓ oz) turnips, chopped
100 g (3⅓ oz) onions, chopped
2 stalks celery, chopped
125 g (4 oz) potatoes, peeled and diced
50 g (1¾ oz) chopped ham
30 g (1 oz) butter

1 teaspoon tomato purée
5 cups (1.25 litres) chicken stock
  (see p. 138)
3 sprigs fresh herbs, chopped
salt and freshly ground pepper
⅔ cup (5 fl oz) cream
chopped watercress for garnish
fried sippets

1. Sauté the vegetables and ham in the butter.
2. Add the tomato purée, stock, herbs, salt and pepper.
3. Simmer for 1½ hours.
4. Cool and rub it through a sieve or purée in a food processor or blender.
5. Heat the purée, add the cream and serve garnished with watercress and sippets.

Friar's Chicken Soup

Serves 6-8

1 kg (2 lb) veal knuckle, cut into
  pieces
8 cups (2 litres) water
1.3 kg (2 lb 10 oz) chicken, cut into
  bite sized pieces

salt and pepper
5 sprigs parsley, chopped
3 eggs, well beaten

1. Simmer the veal, covered, in the water for 2 hours. Strain and save the stock. The veal may be minced and made into meat croquettes.
2. Add the chicken pieces to the boiling stock, season and simmer for 20 minutes.
3. Add two-thirds of the parsley and continue simmering for a further 30 minutes.
4. When the chicken is tender, stir in the eggs, remove from the heat and serve hot sprinkled with the remaining parsley.

Potes Cig

Meat Broth

*This recipe comes from the **Chequers Restaurant** in Clwyd, Wales.*

Serves 6-8

500 g (1 lb) corned (salt) beef
500 g (1 lb) bacon in one piece
250 g (8 oz) carrots, finely chopped
500 g (1 lb) cabbage, finely chopped

250 g (8 oz) swede, finely chopped
1.5 kg (3 lb) potatoes, peeled and cut
  in half
pepper and salt

1. Put the beef, bacon, carrots, cabbage and swede into a saucepan with the pepper and salt. Cover it with water and bring to the boil. Cook for 2 hours or until the meat is almost tender.
2. Add the potatoes and boil for a further 20 minutes.
3. Remove the meat and vegetables from the pan and serve.
4. In Wales, the broth is kept until the next day when it is reheated and served for breakfast poured over small pieces of bread. This dish is called Brwes.

FIRST COURSES

British eating habits changed a great deal during the Victorian era. Early in the 19th century the old, long established system of serving all the cooked dishes at the same time continued. But with the introduction of the style of service called à la Russe, the meal was divided into courses, and while each course may have included several dishes, each dish was served separately.

With the tempo of life increasing this was gradually simplified into the type of service known to us today. There are no hard and fast rules any longer. While in the past no dinner was without soup, nowadays light first course dishes often of fish and seafood might start the dinner.

A simple plate of fresh oysters, sprinkled with lemon juice, or paper-thin slices of smoked Scottish salmon are the ultimate in first courses. However, there are many other tasty dishes to excite the palate at the beginning of a meal. Smoked trout is popular and many rivers and lakes throughout the country are well stocked.

Little puff pastry cases are frequently used often stuffed with kippers, haddock or lobster. Fish and shellfish mousses and creams, seafood in aspic and potted fish are also well liked.

Potted shrimps, originally from Morecombe Bay in Lancashire are a great delicacy and were first made as a means of preserving the surplus catch.

Potting of meats, especially game was also a means of preserving them for the winter. Today, together with game pâtés and terrines, they contribute to the wide range of British first courses.

Smoked Mackerel with Gooseberry Sauce

*This recipe comes from **The Open Arms** in Dirleton in East Lothian, Scotland.*

Serves 4

4 smoked mackerel fillets
4 lettuce leaves
4 lemon wedges

2 tomatoes, cut into wedges
60 g (2 oz) gooseberries, poached
1¼ cups (10 fl oz) cream, lightly whipped

1. Place the mackerel fillets on the lettuce and garnish with lemon and tomato wedges.
2. Finely chop the poached gooseberries (or purée them) and mix with the cream to make a gooseberry sauce. Serve with the mackerel.

The Open Arms, Dirleton

The Open Arms Hotel overlooks the village green and the castle walls and is favoured by golfers who find a number of world famous courses not far from the hotel.

In their restaurant some fine local dishes are served. Fresh Scottish salmon appeared on the table baked in a crispy crust while the Mussel and Onion Stew gave off a tantalising smell. Smoked Mackerel was presented with an unusual sauce made from poached gooseberries and cream.

Right: Clockwise from bottom left: Chicken de Vaux (see p. 42), Smoked Trout (see p. 16), Salmon en Croûte (see p. 30), Cranachan (see p. 80), Mussel and Onion Stew (see p. 32).

Smoked Trout

*From **The Open Arms** in Dirleton, in East Lothian, Scotland.*

Serves 4

4 whole smoked trout
4 large lettuce leaves
4 lemon wedges
2 tomatoes, cut into wedges

1¼ cups (10 fl oz) cream, whipped
30 g (1 oz) grated horse-radish
mustard and cress for garnish

1. Skin the trout and place on the lettuce leaves.
2. Garnish with lemon and tomato wedges.
3. Mix the cream and horse-radish and serve separately.
4. Decorate with mustard and cress.

Potted Duck

*From **Chequers Inn**, Fowlermere, Near Royston*

meat and liver from one duckling
250 g (8 oz) finely minced veal
½ cup (2 oz) dry breadcrumbs
2 tablespoons finely chopped onion
1 tablespoon finely chopped chervil
3 sprigs parsley, finely chopped

salt and freshly ground pepper
grated rind from half an orange
2 tablespoons brandy or dry sherry
2 eggs, lightly beaten
2-3 slices bacon

1. Preheat oven to 160°C (325°F/Gas 3).
2. Finely mince the duck meat and liver.
3. Mix it with the veal, breadcrumbs, onion, chervil, parsley, salt and pepper.
4. Stir in the orange rind, brandy or sherry and eggs.
5. Spoon into a greased terrine dish and cover with bacon.
6. Bake in a baking tin half filled with hot water for 1¾ hours.
7. Remove from the oven, allow to cool and refrigerate overnight. Serve at room temperature with hot buttered toast.

Kipper Cheese Puffs

Serves 8

300 g (10 oz) kipper fillets
30 g (1 oz) butter
¼ cup (1 oz) flour
1¼ cups (10 fl oz) hot milk
½ cup (2 oz) grated Lancashire cheese

salt and freshly ground pepper
375 g (12 oz) defrosted puff pastry
1 egg, lightly beaten
lemon wedges for garnish

1. Preheat oven to 220°C (425°F/Gas 7).
2. Poach the fillets in water for 2 to 3 minutes, drain, save the water. Skin the fillets, remove all bones and chop the flesh into small pieces.
3. In a saucepan melt the butter, add the flour and cook for a few minutes without colouring.
4. Stir in the milk and if it looks too thick add a little of the poaching liquid. Cook for a few minutes stirring continuously.
5. Remove from the heat, stir in the cheese and the kippers, season and let it cool.
6. Roll out the pastry 25 x 50 cm (10 x 20 inches) and cut it into eight pieces 12½ cm (5 inches) square.
7. Place the pastry on a greased baking tray and put a portion of the kipper mixture on each.
8. Brush the edges with the egg, fold the square into a triangle and seal the edges firmly.
9. Brush them with egg and bake for approximately 20 minutes or until golden brown.

Oysters on Skewers

Serves 6

36 oysters
3 sweetbreads, cut into small chunks
6 bacon slices, cut into short strips
3 sprigs parsley, chopped
3 spring onions (scallions), chopped

¼ teaspoon ground thyme
salt and freshly ground pepper
2 eggs, lightly beaten
½ cup (2 oz) dry breadcrumbs
oil for frying

1. Keep the liquid from the oysters and thread them onto six skewers, alternating with sweetbreads and bacon.
2. Sprinkle the skewers with parsley, spring onions, thyme, salt and pepper.
3. Dip them in the eggs, coat them with breadcrumbs and shallow fry them in the hot oil.
4. Serve them with chunks of fresh crusty bread and a Béchamel sauce (see p. 140) made with the oyster liquid instead of milk.

Poached Eggs on Anchovy Toast

Serves 6

2½ cups (20 fl oz) milk
1 bay leaf
1 sprig each of thyme and marjoram
1 pinch each of mace and pepper
8 anchovy fillets
30 g (1 oz) soft butter

1 tablespoon oil
2 tablespoons dry sherry
1 egg yolk
6 slices fried bread
6 eggs

1. Boil the milk with the bay leaf, thyme, marjoram, mace and pepper. Remove from the heat, cover and let it stand for one hour.
2. Mash the anchovies together with the butter, oil, sherry and egg yolk.
3. Coat the bread with the anchovy mixture.
4. Strain the milk, bring it to boiling point, then reduce the heat and poach the eggs in it.
5. Arrange the eggs on the toast and serve immediately.

Wyau Mon

Anglesey Eggs

*From the **King's Head Hotel** in Monmouth, Wales.*

Serves 4

8 eggs
750 g (1½ lb) potatoes,
    peeled and cut into quarters
6 leeks, washed
knob of butter

Cheese Sauce
30 g (1 oz) butter
¼ cup (1 oz) flour
1¼ cups (10 fl oz) milk
90 g (3 oz) Caerphilly cheese, grated

1. Hard-boil the eggs, shell them and leave them in a bowl of cold water.
2. Boil the potatoes, strain and mash them.
3. Slice the leeks into thin rings and boil them in salted water for 10 minutes. Drain.
4. Add the leeks to the mashed potato with the knob of butter and beat well.
5. To make the sauce, melt the butter in a saucepan, add the flour and stir to make a roux. Add the milk and cook the sauce, whisking constantly with a wire whisk, until it is smooth. Add 75 g of the cheese and cook for a few minutes longer.
6. Preheat the oven to 200°C (400°F/Gas 6).
7. Place the potato mixture on the bottom and around the sides of a warmed ovenproof dish. Cut the eggs in half lengthwise and put them, cut side down, in the centre of the dish.
8. Coat the eggs with the sauce and sprinkle with the remaining grated cheese.
9. Cook in the oven for 20 minutes or until the top is golden.

Right: A cobblestone lane in Ledbury in the county of Hereford and Worcester.

Seafood Puffs

*This recipe comes from the **Parkend Restaurant** in Wigton, Cumbria.*
The Parkend has an informal country atmosphere and a reputation for local dishes served in friendly surroundings. If some of the dishes they prepared for me are an indication, their reputation is fully justified. Their baked gammon, cooked in cider and served with Cumberland Sauce, was very tasty, and their Cumberland Rum Nicky was a delicious dessert.

Serves 6-8

Choux Paste
150 ml (5 fl oz) water
75 g (2½ oz) butter
½ teaspoon sugar
1 cup (4 oz) flour
4 large eggs

Filling
500 g (1 lb) cooked prawns or
  500-750 g (1-1½ lb) lobster or
  500-750 g (1-1½ lb) crab
2 cups (16 fl oz) milk

1 bay leaf/1 small onion, peeled
125 g (4 oz) butter
½ cup (2 oz) flour
2 egg yolks
2 tablespoons cream
2 teaspoons grated cheese
1 tablespoon sherry
125 g (4 oz) button mushrooms, finely sliced
1 clove garlic, crushed
salt and pepper
parsley

Puffs:
1. Put the water, butter and sugar into a pan and bring to the boil.
2. Remove from the heat and immediately tip in the sieved flour.
3. Return to the heat and beat with a wooden spoon until the dough leaves the sides of the pan.
4. Leave to cool for 5 minutes, then beat in the eggs one at a time.
5. Preheat the oven to 240°C (475°F/Gas 9).
6. Pipe the mixture in small heaps on to a baking sheet lined with kitchen parchment leaving plenty of room between each for the puffs to expand. Invert a metal biscuit tin over the top to allow the puffs to cook in their own steam.
7. Bake for 25 minutes, then raise the tin to check the puffs. If they are not brown enough, cook them, without the biscuit tin, for a further 3 minutes.
8. With a sharp knife, slit the sides of the puffs and leave in the turned off oven with the door slightly open, to dry off.

Filling:
1. Peel the shellfish and simmer the shells and milk in a pan with the bay leaf and onion for 15 minutes.
2. In a separate pan, melt half the butter, add the flour, stir well then gradually add the strained milk, stirring until the mixture is smooth.
3. Mix the egg yolks with the cream and add it to the sauce, then add the cheese and sherry.
4. Melt the remaining butter in another pan with the garlic and gently cook the mushrooms for a few minutes.
5. Add these to the sauce with the chopped shellfish, salt, pepper and parsley.
6. Heat the sauce gently, without boiling, then split the puffs, fill with the sauce and serve at once as a first course.

Potted Silloth Shrimps

*From **The Pheasant Inn** on Bassenthwaite Lake in Cumberland.*
Potting shrimps is an old way of preserving a surplus catch. Those from Morecombe have been well known for their delicate flavour since the 18th century.

Serves 2

125 g (4 oz) brown 'Silloth' shrimps
  (or small raw prawns)
60 g (2 oz) butter

salt and black pepper
1 tablespoon dry white wine

1. Bring a large pan of salted water to the boil. Drop in the shrimps and boil for 3 minutes.
2. Plunge the shrimps immediately into cold water, then shell and devein them.
3. Put the shrimps into a bowl and sprinkle them with the wine. Leave to marinate for 1 hour.
4. Force the shrimps into small pots and top each one with a layer of butter. Chill until needed.
5. Serve on a bed of lettuce with tomato, cucumber, watercress, lemon wedges and thin slices of brown bread and butter.

Asparagus and Game Mousse

*From **The George Hotel** in Chollerford, Northumberland.*
The George Hotel is situated on the banks of the river North Tyne, 4 miles north of the market town of Hexham in the village of Chollerford. It is a convenient staging point to the surrounding countryside. The famous and ancient Roman Wall is one of the attractions of the area.
The restaurant, which overlooks the river and old stone bridge, serves a wide range of dishes. Some local or regional fare appears on the menu: spiced beef, pease pudding and crown of lamb are amongst them. Asparagus and game mousse are a speciality and in the apple and bramble fool, apples and blackberries combine in a tasty mixture.

Serves 4-6

2½ cups (20 fl oz) water
1 tablespoon gelatine, softened in a
  little cold water
125 g (4 oz) fresh cooked asparagus,
  chopped, plus extra cooked
  asparagus tips for garnish

250 g (8 oz) cooked pheasant or guinea
  fowl, minced
1 cup (8 fl oz) cream
salt
freshly ground black pepper

1. Bring the water to the boil and add the gelatine. Stir until it has dissolved. Add the asparagus and game, stirring well. Set the mixture aside to cool to lukewarm.
2. Add the cream, salt and pepper and pour the mixture into a mould. Refrigerate until set.
3. Remove the mousse from the mould and decorate with asparagus tips.

VEGETABLES

Vegetables have been cultivated in the British Isles since early days. The vegetable and herb gardens of mediaeval monasteries and manor houses were works of art and until the 18th and early 19th century almost everybody grew their own. However, the increasing population in the industrial towns created a demand which could not be satisfied by the garden plot around the house. This gave rise to the first market gardens where vegetables were grown for sale rather than for personal consumption.

Originally the range of vegetables was quite limited: onions, cabbage, garlic, leeks, peas and beans — which were also dried to last through the winter months — were the only ones available. Gradually, as new types of vegetables were introduced, the variety grew and today, except for vegetables from warmer climates, most are grown in Britain.

Vegetables have always played an important role in providing nourishment. While in the Middle Ages meat and fish were the privilege of the rich, the peasant and poor townfolk relied to a very large extent on vegetables for their sustenance. Vegetables were used to stretch what little meat was available and today vegetables are still used as the basis for stews much more frequently than in their own right.

In Britain there is little regional variation in the preparation of vegetables and only a few, such as potatoes or leeks, are more typical of some parts than others.

Parsnips, Potatoes and Bacon

Serves 6

500 g (1 lb) parsnips, peeled and diced
500 g (1 lb) potatoes, peeled and thickly sliced
250 g (8 oz) bacon slices, chopped

1¼ cups (10 fl oz) chicken stock (see p. 138)
salt and freshly ground pepper

1. Preheat oven to 180°C (350°F/Gas 4).
2. Mix parsnips, potatoes and bacon together and place them in a greased ovenproof dish.
3. Add the stock, salt and pepper.
4. Cover the dish and bake for one hour or until vegetables are tender. Serve with grilled or roast meat.

Right: A selection of British vegetables and herbs.

Northumbrian Leek Pudding

Serves 6

1.75 kg (3½ lb) suet pastry (see p.141)
1.25 kg (2½ lb) leeks, cleaned and chopped

125 g (4 oz) butter
salt and freshly ground pepper

1. Line a 1.5 litre (3 pt) pudding basin with three-quarters of the suet pastry.
2. Fill the basin with leeks, dot with butter and season with salt and pepper.
3. Cover with the rest of the pastry, tie down with foil and place the basin in a saucepan half-filled with water. Cover and steam it for 2 hours. Traditionally, this is served with stews.

Welsh Onion Cake

Serves 6

1 kg (2 lb) potatoes, peeled and sliced
250 g (8 oz) onions, finely chopped

90 g (3 oz) butter, melted
salt and freshly ground pepper

1. Preheat the oven to 190°C (375°F/Gas 5).
2. Grease an 18 cm (7 inch) soufflé dish and place a layer of potatoes on the bottom and then a layer of onions, dot with butter and sprinkle with salt and pepper.
3. Repeat the layers, finishing off with potatoes. Brush with butter and bake for 1 to 1¼ hours.
4. Turn out and serve hot.

Braised Celery with Apples

Serves 4

250 g (8 oz) cooking apples, peeled and diced
4 cloves
1½ tablespoons (1 oz) sugar

8 slices bacon
1 bunch celery, cut into 7.5-10 cm (3-4 inch) pieces
salt and freshly ground pepper

1. Preheat the oven to 180°C (350°F/Gas 4).
2. Put the apples with a little water in a saucepan, add the cloves and sugar and cook until soft.
3. Rub the apples through a sieve.
4. Cover the bottom of a casserole with half the bacon and top it with the apple purée.
5. Arrange the celery on top, sprinkle it with salt and pepper and cover it with bacon.
6. Place a lid on the casserole and bake it for 1½ hours.

Devonshire Stew

Serves 8

1 kg (2 lb) mashed potatoes
500 g (1 lb) shredded boiled cabbage
500 g (1 lb) boiled chopped onions

salt and freshly ground pepper
100 g (3½ oz) butter

1. Combine the potatoes with the cabbage and onions and season with salt and pepper.
2. In a large frying pan or casserole, melt the butter and fry the mixture until brown. Serve hot.

Pease Pudding

*This recipe comes from **The George Hotel** in Chollerford, Northumberland.*
A dish which dates back to the Middle Ages and was originally known as pease porridge. It is really a pea purée which is served with pickled pork or boiled beef.

Serves 4-6

250 g (8 oz) yellow split peas
4 cups (1 litre) stock made from ham or bacon bones, heated

salt
freshly ground black pepper

1. Place the peas in a muslin bag allowing plenty of room for them to swell up. Put the bag into the pan of hot stock and leave them to soak for 3 hours.
2. Bring the stock (with the bag of peas) to the boil, then simmer for about 45 minutes or until the peas are soft.
3. Remove the peas from the bag and place them into a bowl. Beat them with a wooden spoon until they are creamy.
4. Reheat them for a few minutes over low heat and serve immediately with salted meat.

Potato Cakes

*From the **Waterside Restaurant** in Romiley, Manchester.*

Serves 4

250 g (8 oz) cooked, cold potatoes
15 g (½ oz) butter, melted
½ teaspoon salt

½ cup (2 oz) flour or fine oatmeal
½ teaspoon baking powder

1. Mash the potatoes and add butter and salt.
2. Work in as much flour mixed with baking powder as you need to make a pliable dough.
3. Roll it out thinly, cut in rounds with a bread and butter plate and then mark into quarters.
4. Prick with a fork and cook on a hot griddle for 5 minutes each side.
5. Serve with plenty of butter.

Waterside Restaurant, Romiley, Stockport, Greater Manchester

Dine by candlelight in the authentic atmosphere of an old world cottage are the words on the card.

The two-hundred-year-old restaurant with its oak beams, is on the edge of the Cheshire Ring canal and when I arrived there it was packed for lunch. I guess it is not surprising as Greater Manchester is not really known as a gourmet centre and there are very few good eating places in the region. Monty Small, the proprietor and chef is dedicated to good food. Lancashire steak pie may not sound very grand but as prepared by Monty, it is very tasty.

Hindle Wakes Chicken is an unusual combination of chicken, prunes and spices and is a typical Lancashire dish.

As dessert, Chester Pudding is certainly a regional dish but Monty Small's Tipsy Hedgehog is not only great to look at but delicious to eat. I suspect it is his own creation but who cares when it is a great dish to finish a meal.

***Right:** Clockwise from top left: Lancashire Steak Pie (see p. 72), Hindle Wakes Chicken (see p. 44), Tipsy Hedgehog (see p. 94), Pea and Bacon Rib Soup (see p. 12).*

Wyau Yns Mon

Anglesey Mushrooms

*From **The Chequers** in Northophall Village in Clwyd, Wales.*

Serves 2

125 g (4 oz) button mushrooms,
  stems chopped
1¼ cups (10 fl oz) Béchamel sauce
  (see p. 140)
1 small clove garlic, crushed

1 large potato, peeled,
  boiled and mashed with butter
2 thick slices bread, toasted

1. Add the mushrooms to the Béchamel sauce and simmer for 5 minutes.
2. Add the garlic and cook for a further 2 minutes.
3. Preheat the grill (broiler) to high.
4. Place each slice of toast on a large heatproof plate and pipe mashed potato around the toast.
5. Pour the mushroom Béchamel over the toast and put the plates under the hot grill. It is ready to serve when the potato browns.

Bacon Floddies

*From the **Bush Hotel** at Farnham in Surrey.*
Bacon floddies are a variation of potato floddies which are known in many parts of the country. Grated cheese, chopped herbs, minced or sausage meat, can be added to the batter and it can be served as a light supper dish.

Serves 2-3

1 large potato, peeled and grated
1 small onion, finely chopped
60 g (2 oz) bacon,
  rinds removed and finely chopped
30 g (1 oz) mushrooms, finely chopped

pinch thyme
salt
pepper
1 egg, beaten
dripping or oil for frying

1. Place potato, onion, bacon, mushrooms, thyme, salt and pepper in a bowl and mix in the egg.
2. Heat 1 cm (½ inch) dripping or oil in a frying pan and drop large spoonfuls of the mixture into it.
3. Fry over low heat, turning once.
4. Serve hot with mustard pickle.

Parsnip Cakes

Serves 6

1 kg (2 lb) boiled and mashed parsnips
1 cup (4 oz) flour
salt and freshly ground pepper
60 g (2 oz) butter, melted

2 eggs, lightly beaten
½ cup (2 oz) dry breadcrumbs
oil for frying

1. Mix the parsnips with half the flour, the salt and pepper.
2. Add the butter and knead the mixture into a dough.
3. Form it into round flat cakes, dust them with the remaining flour, dip them in the egg and coat them with breadcrumbs.
4. Heat the oil and fry them on both sides until golden brown.

Tomatoes Stuffed with Stilton

Serves 4

4 large tomatoes
salt and freshly ground pepper
30 g (1 oz) softened butter

1 tablespoon chopped chives
125 g (4 oz) crumbled Stilton cheese

1. Dip the tomatoes in boiling water for 20 to 30 seconds and peel them.
2. Cut off the tops and squeeze out the pips.
3. Scoop out the flesh, chop it and mix it with the salt, pepper, butter, chives and cheese.
4. Put the mixture into the tomatoes, cover with the lids and refrigerate. Serve as a salad.

FISH

The waters around the British Isles abound with fish and seafood of all types and in many of the coastal countries regional fish dishes can be found.

In the days before transportation and refrigeration — introduced at the beginning of the 19th century — changed fish-eating habits, fresh seafood did not reach far inland. However, preserving fish by salting, drying or smoking was practised for many centuries and this enabled the inland parts of the country to participate to a limited extent in the harvest of the sea.

While large parts of the country were deprived of fresh ocean fish, there was plenty of freshwater fish available from rivers, lakes and ponds. Today the situation is quite different: fresh fish and seafood can be found even in the remotest parts of the land, while catching river and lake fish, except for the salmon and trout, has become the preserve of the amateur.

Some of the best seafood is caught off the rough coast of Cornwall and it is not surprising to find many good fish dishes in that region. Pilchards which are caught here in large quantities finish up in the unusual Stargazy Pie (p. 77) while Cornish lobsters are among the best. The Welsh do tasty things with herrings, kippers, mackerel, cockles and mussels.

Cod, especially in the salted form has been popular for centuries. So has haddock. Much used in Scottish cooking, the Scottish smoked haddock is well known. The Scots have developed a very tasty way of preserving herrings by splitting them open, cleaning them and immersing them in a highly concentrated brine which coats the herring and dries to a golden shine while being smoked.

The Dover sole is undoubtedly the most noble of fish caught in British waters and has graced many an elegant dinner table.

Among freshwater fish this distinction goes to salmon which has been called the king of fish. Cut into steaks, grilled or fried and served with a variety of garnishes its flavour and texture is unsurpassed. The best are caught in Scotland and Scottish smoked salmon is the best in the world.

Most fish and seafood is prepared simply. However, the most typically British seafood dishes are fish pies and puddings, fish pastes and potted fish.

Salmon en Croûte

*From **The Open Arms** in Dirleton in East Lothian, Scotland.*

Serves 4-6

1 salmon or a large trout	**egg wash (1 egg yolk, mixed with a**
6 asparagus tips, steamed for 5 minutes	**little**
6 slices streaky (fat) bacon	**cold water)**
puff pastry	**lettuce, tomato, cucumber**
	and lemon to garnish

1. Preheat the oven to 180°C (350° F/Gas 4).
2. Remove the head and tail of the fish and cut along the backbone until you have two sides of boneless salmon. Skin both sides.
3. Fill the centre of the salmon with asparagus, put the two sides together and wrap in bacon.
4. Roll out the puff pastry and wrap the fish in it. Brush with eggwash.
5. Bake for 30 to 40 minutes or until the pastry is golden brown and the fish is cooked. Leave it to cool.
6. Serve it cut into slices with lettuce, tomato, cucumber and wedges of lemon.

Right: Fresh trout.

Mussel and Onion Stew

*From **The Open Arms** in Dirleton in East Lothian, Scotland.*
It's an ancient Scottish dish dating back to the Middle Ages.

Serves 4

90 g (3 oz) butter
1 large onion, sliced
½ cup (2 oz) flour
2½ cups (20 fl oz) fish stock (see p. 139)
salt and black pepper

750 g (1½ lb) mussels, shelled
1 cup (8 fl oz) white wine
3 tablespoons cream
1 tablespoon fresh parsley,
  finely chopped
pinch of dried mixed herbs

1. Melt the butter in a pan and add the onion. Cook over gentle heat until the onion is soft.
2. Add the flour, stir well, then add the fish stock. Stir until smooth and then simmer for a few minutes.
3. Add the mussels and white wine, bring to the boil then simmer for about 10 minutes.
4. Add the cream, parsley and herbs and serve in an earthenware or porcelain terrine.

Brithyll yr Afon gyda Chig Moch
Trout with Bacon

*This recipe comes from **The Chequers** in Clwyd, Wales.*

Serves 4

4 small trout, split and cleaned
500 g (1 lb) spinach, well washed
½ cup (3 oz) raisins

4 slices bacon
2 tablespoons melted butter

1. Cook the spinach in very little water for 6 to 8 minutes. Drain it well and chop it finely.
2. Mix the raisins into the spinach and add a knob of butter.
3. Stuff each trout with a little of this mixture and brush their skins with melted butter.
4. Grill the trout for 5 minutes each side.
5. A few minutes before the trout are ready, grill the bacon slices.
6. Serve the trout and bacon together.

Sewin (Sea Trout) Baked in butter with Sorrel Sauce

Sewin is a delicious pink firm-fleshed fish, believed by many connoisseurs to be as good as or better than salmon. If it is not available, fresh-water trout may be used.
*This recipe comes from **Ty Mawr** in Brechfa, Wales.*
Run by Cliff and Jill Ross, the Ty Mawr is a 16th century house which has been converted into a small comfortable hotel. Its setting in a picturesque, Welsh-speaking village on the banks of the Marlais is very pretty.

*   While the restaurant specialises in Cordon Bleu cooking, local Welsh food is also served. I tried laver soup, made from purple coloured edible seaweed which had been gathered by my hosts at low tide. Faggots, which is pig's liver, sometimes cooked in a pig's caul – in the 19th century it was jokingly called poor man's goose – was formed into small balls and baked in the oven.*

Serves 4-6

1 large or 2 smaller trout	*Sorrel Sauce*
1 tablespoon butter, melted	**60 g (2 oz) butter**
1 large onion, chopped	**3 spring onions (scallions), finely chopped**
2 bay leaves, crumbled	
salt and pepper	**250 g (8 oz) fresh sorrel, chopped**
pinch of dried dill	**½ cup (2 oz) flour**
sea salt	**1¼ cups (10 fl oz) chicken stock (see p. 138)**
1 cup (8 fl oz) dry white wine	**½ teaspoon sugar**
	salt and pepper

1. Preheat the oven to 190°C (375°F/Gas 5).
2. Brush a large sheet of foil with melted butter and place the cleaned trout in the centre.
3. Stuff the cavity with the onion, bay leaves, salt and pepper.
4. Rub the skin with sea salt.
5. Add the wine and loosely wrap the fish in the foil. Place it in a baking dish and bake for 10 minutes per 500 g.
6. When it is cooked, remove it from the oven but leave it wrapped in foil for a further 20 minutes.
7. To make the sauce, melt the butter and cook the spring onions and sorrel in it over low heat for 10 minutes.
8. Stir in the flour and add the stock, sugar and seasoning. Cook for a further 20 minutes.
9. Put the sauce through a blender or food processor until it is smooth and creamy.
10. Return it to the pan and reheat it gently.
11. When the fish has finished cooking, carefully remove the skin and remove the light-brown bits near the head with a knife.
12. Serve the fish and the sauce separately.

Note: The fish may also be served cold. In this case, cool the sauce and mix it with 1 cup (8 fl oz) of mayonnaise.

Trout Agincourt

*From the **King's Head** in Monmouth, Wales.*

Serves 4

4 trout, cleaned and heads removed
1 tablespoon seasoned flour
1 egg, beaten
2 tablespoons dry breadcrumbs
oil for deep frying

Forcemeat
30 g (1 oz) butter
1 onion, finely chopped
60 g (2 oz) mushrooms, finely chopped
1 teaspoon dried dill
125 g (4 oz) prawns, peeled,
  deveined and finely chopped
1 cup (2 oz) fresh white breadcrumbs
salt and pepper
1 egg yolk

1. Coat the trout in the flour, then the egg and breadcrumbs and deep fry in the hot oil for a few minutes only — just until they are golden brown. Remove them and drain them on kitchen paper.
2. To make the forcemeat, melt the butter in a frying pan and add the onion, mushrooms and dill. Fry for about 5 minutes, until the onion is soft, but not brown. Add the prawns and cook for a few minutes longer.
3. Add the breadcrumbs and season with salt and pepper.
4. Remove the pan from the heat and bind the forcemeat together with the egg yolk.
5. Spoon some of this mixture into the cavity of each trout.
6. Preheat the oven to 180°C (350°F/Gas 4).
7. Lay the trout in an oiled baking dish and bake for 10 to 15 minutes or until cooked through.
8. Serve garnished with lemon wedges, parsley and cooked king prawns.

The Anglers' Rest, Fingle Bridge, Exeter

The Anglers' Rest is what poets write about: an unspoiled woodland setting by a sparkling salmon and trout river, a romantic stone bridge, heather-covered hills, surrounded by scenery unchanged for hundreds of years.

Here in the house dating back to Elizabethan times not far from the Dartmoor National Park, typical Devonshire fare is served to the hungry traveller: cider-baked pork chops, beefsteak and kidney pie, baked Devonshire apple dumplings, Devon apple cake and Devonshire junket. All of this washed down with local cider.

It's simple fare but apples, cider and the frequent use of cream give it a characteristic, rich flavour.

Mine hosts Jack and Elsie Price continue an eighty-year-old family tradition of catering for the hungry traveller.

Cornish Roast Lobsters

*This recipe dates back to 1727. It comes from **The Coachmakers Arms** in Callington, Cornwall.*

Cornwall is famous for its harvest of the sea. Some of the best fish in the country come from the many fishing villages dotted along the rugged coast.

Serves 4

1 small onion, chopped
1 cup (8 fl oz) water
1 cup (8 fl oz) white wine vinegar
bouquet garni, consisting of
   1 sprig fresh thyme, 3 sprigs fresh
   parsley and 1 bay leaf tied up
   with string
pepper
salt
2 live lobsters

Sauce
30 g (1 oz) butter
1 small tin anchovy fillets, drained
   and chopped
1 cup (8 fl oz) white wine
1 tablespoon lemon juice or white wine
   vinegar
pinch of grated nutmeg
pinch of ground mace
pepper
¼ cup (½ oz) fresh breadcrumbs

1. Preheat the oven to 180°C (350°F/Gas 4).
2. Put the onion, water, vinegar, bouquet garni, pepper and salt in a pan and bring it to the boil. Simmer for 5 minutes.
3. Wash the lobsters and roast them on a spit in the oven or in a baking dish for ¾ hour, basting them frequently with the above mixture.
4. Meanwhile, make the sauce. Melt the butter in a pan and add the anchovies, mashing them well with a wooden spoon.
5. Add the wine, lemon juice, nutmeg, mace and pepper and simmer, stirring occasionally, for 5 minutes.
6. Stir in the breadcrumbs and simmer for a few minutes longer.
7. Remove the lobsters from the oven, split them, remove their intestines, crack the claws and serve with the hot sauce.

Essex Whitebait in Batter

Serves 4

1 cup (4 oz) flour
pinch of salt
1 egg, lightly beaten
⅔ cup (5 fl oz) milk
500 g (1 lb) whitebait

flour
salt, freshly ground pepper
oil for deep frying
lemon wedges and parsley sprigs
   for garnish

1. Make a batter by combining the flour, salt, egg and milk, and leave it to rest for 30 minutes before using it.
2. Dust the whitebait with seasoned flour.
3. Dip the fish in the batter and deep fry in hot oil until golden brown.
4. Serve hot garnished with lemon wedges and parsley.

Dover Sole in Cider

*From the **Bush Hotel** in Farnham, Surrey.*
Dover sole has the reputation of being the finest of all flat-type fish. It is delicate and has a flavour which distinguishes it from other similar looking fish such as lemon sole or flounder. The recipe given here is quite elaborate, however, Dover sole, simply grilled and served with lemon butter can be equally enjoyable.

Serves 4

4 spring onions (scallions), finely chopped
8 fillets of Dover sole (or John Dory) weighing about 90 g (3 oz) each
pinch of dried rosemary
salt
pepper

2 cups (16 fl oz) cider
¼ cup (1 oz) grated Cheddar cheese
¼ cup (2 fl oz) cream
1 egg
1 tablespoon finely chopped parsley
mashed potatoes for serving

1. Preheat the oven to 180°C (350°F/Gas 4).
2. Sprinkle half the chopped spring onions on the bottom of an ovenproof casserole.
3. Tuck under the 2 ends of the fish fillets and lay them on the onions.
4. Sprinkle with the remaining onions, the rosemary, salt and pepper and pour over the cider.
5. Bake for 15 minutes.
6. Remove the fish with a slotted spoon, place them on a serving dish and sprinkle them with cheese.
7. Reduce the cooking liquid to about half its original volume by fast boiling.
8. Beat the cream and egg together, add a little of the hot cooking liquid to it, then return it to the pan, stirring constantly and making sure it doesn't boil.
9. When it has thickened slightly, pour it over the fish.
10. Glaze under a hot grill, sprinkle with parsley and serve surrounded by piped mashed potato.

John Dory in White Wine

Serves 4

8 fillets of John Dory
¾ cup (6 fl oz) dry white wine
juice of 1 lemon

salt and freshly ground pepper
3 tablespoons olive oil
finely chopped parsley

1. In a large frying pan gently poach the fish in wine, lemon juice, salt and pepper for 2 to 3 minutes.
2. Leave the fish to cool in the liquid.
3. Serve it chilled, sprinkled with a dressing made from two parts of the cooking liquid to one part oil seasoned with salt and pepper and sprinkled with parsley.

Fillets of Sole with Oysters

Serves 4

50 g (1¾ oz) spring onions (scallions), chopped
2 sprigs thyme, chopped
3 sprigs parsley, chopped
juice of ½ lemon
8 fillets of sole, flounder or John Dory
12 oysters

125 g (4 oz) tomatoes, peeled, quartered and seeded
⅔ cup (5 fl oz) dry white wine
½ cup (4 fl oz) fish stock (see p. 139)
salt and freshly ground pepper
125 g (4 oz) butter
3 sprigs parsley, finely chopped

1. Preheat the oven to 180°C (350° F/Gas 4).
2. Mix the onions, thyme, parsley and lemon juice and spread it over the bottom of a shallow, buttered oven dish.
3. Arrange the fish fillets on top and garnish them with oysters and tomatoes.
4. Add the wine and stock and sprinkle with salt and pepper.
5. Cover with aluminium foil and bake in the preheated oven for about 30 minutes.
6. Carefully remove the fillets with the tomatoes and oysters to a serving dish and keep them warm.
7. Strain the cooking liquid into a saucepan and reduce it over high heat to a glaze.
8. Remove it from the heat and gradually beat in the butter. Add the parsley, season to taste, pour the sauce over the fish and serve hot with boiled new potatoes.

Somerset Casserole

Serves 4

500 g (1 lb) firm white fish, cut into small cubes
salt and freshly ground pepper
100 g (3⅓ oz) button mushrooms, sliced
2 tomatoes, peeled and sliced
¾ cup (6 fl oz) cider

50 g (1¾ oz) butter
¼ cup (1 oz) flour
250 g (8 oz) seasoned mashed potatoes
tomato slices and parsley sprigs for garnish
½ cup (2 oz) grated cheese

1. Preheat oven to 190°C (375°F/Gas 5).
2. Place the fish in a shallow buttered ovenproof dish and season with salt and pepper.
3. Cover with mushrooms and tomatoes, add the cider and dot with half of the butter.
4. Cover with aluminium foil and cook in the preheated oven for 20 minutes.
5. Strain the cooking liquid and reserve it.
6. Melt the remaining butter, add the flour and cook without colouring for 2 to 3 minutes and then add the cooking liquid. Cook for 2 to 3 minutes.
7. Pour the sauce over the fish and pipe a border of potatoes on top.
8. Increase the oven temperature to 230°C (450° F/Gas 8). Garnish the top with tomato slices, sprinkle it with cheese and bake until the top is brown.
9. Serve garnished with parsley.

Right: Cambridge, the tranquil waters of the Backs.

Stuffed Bream

Serves 4

150 g (5 oz) white fish fillets, finely chopped
15 g (½ oz) softened butter
¼ cup (1 oz) dry breadcrumbs
2 anchovy fillets, finely chopped
3-4 oysters (optional)
1 teaspoon chopped fresh or dried mixed herbs

1 egg lightly beaten
salt and freshly ground pepper
4 small bream, scaled and cleaned
flour
butter

1. Preheat oven to 180°C (350° F/Gas 4).
2. To make the stuffing, combine and mix well together the chopped fish fillets, butter, breadcrumbs, anchovies, oysters, herbs, egg, salt and pepper.
3. Divide the stuffing into 4 equal parts and place it in the cavities of the fish.
4. Sprinkle the fish with flour, salt and pepper and place them in a shallow ovenproof dish.
5. Dot them with butter, cover the dish with foil and bake in the preheated oven for 40 to 45 minutes.

Fried Scallops

Serves 4

1 tablespoon olive oil
juice of ½ lemon
salt and freshly ground pepper
3 sprigs parsley, chopped
12-16 scallops
75 g (2½ oz) ham, finely chopped
½ cup (2 oz) dry breadcrumbs

2 tablespoons grated Parmesan cheese
1 small onion, finely chopped
flour
1-2 eggs, lightly beaten
oil for deep frying
lettuce leaves and lemon wedges

1. Combine the oil, lemon juice, salt, pepper and parsley and marinate the scallops in the mixture for 30 to 45 minutes.
2. Combine the ham, breadcrumbs, cheese, onions, salt and pepper.
3. Drain the scallops, dust them with flour, dip them in the egg and coat them with the ham-breadcrumb mixture.
4. Deep-fry them in the heated oil until golden brown.
5. Serve on lettuce leaves garnished with lemon wedges.

Mousse of Smoked Haddock

Serves 6

2 large smoked haddock fillets
15 g (½ oz) butter
1 tablespoon flour
⅔ cup (5 fl oz) hot milk
pinch of salt and pepper

⅔ cup (5 fl oz) cream
⅔ cup (5 fl oz) dry white wine, heated
2 teaspoons gelatine
2 egg whites, stiffly beaten
salt and pepper

1. Simmer the fish in water until the flesh is soft and cooked.
2. Remove the skin and bones. In a mincer, blender or food processor, reduce the flesh to a paste.
3. To make a Béchamel sauce, melt the butter, stir in the flour and cook without browning for 2 minutes. Add the milk and mix it to a smooth consistency, cook for 2 to 3 minutes and season.
4. Add the fish paste to the sauce.
5. Melt the gelatine in a little water, mix it into the hot wine and stir it into the fish mixture.
6. Mix in the cream and season to taste but take care not to over-salt it as the haddock is already salty.
7. Fold in the egg whites.
8. Spoon the mixture into individual moulds or one large one. Refrigerate for a few hours. To serve, turn out the mousse and serve it with a salad and buttered toast.

Trout with Lemon Cucumber Butter

*From the **Cavendish Hotel**, Baslow, Bakewell, Derbyshire*

Serves 4

4 trout
½ cup (2 oz) seasoned flour
juice of 1 lemon
2 sprigs thyme, finely chopped
125 g (4 oz) butter, melted

Lemon Cucumber Butter
125 g (4 oz) softened butter
100 g (3⅓ oz) cucumber, finely
  chopped, peeled and seeded
juice of 1 lemon
grated rind of 1 lemon
salt and freshly ground pepper

1. Preheat oven to 200°C (400°F/Gas 6).
2. Roll the trout in seasoned flour and sprinkle the inside with some of the lemon juice and the thyme.
3. Place the trout in a baking dish and pour the rest of the lemon juice and the melted butter over it.
4. Place it in the preheated oven and bake for 8 to 10 minutes, turning it once.
5. To serve, place it on a serving dish with the lemon cucumber butter.
6. To make the lemon cucumber butter, mix the ingredients together, roll it in aluminium foil, refrigerate until firm and cut into slices to serve.

POULTRY AND GAME BIRDS

Today a farmyard chicken is a rare bird. Brought into the world in an incubator and reared scientifically on a standard diet of processed food, it grows up plump and tender but deprived of the flavoursome meat its farmyard cousins in olden days offered.

Poultry has not played a very important part at the tables of a basically meat-eating people so it is not surprising that there is no great variety of interesting recipes in the British cooking repertoire.

In the past, cooks relied on the natural flavour of the range-run birds and did not venture very far beyond the simple roast chicken.

There are also not many regional variations and whenever a place name occurs in the name of the dish, it usually refers to the origin of the birds, as for example in Aylesbury Duck.

As in many other countries, in England the goose is a festive bird. Guinea fowl, once a game bird, is now raised for the table.

Other game birds such as wild duck, pheasant, quail, pigeon and especially partridge are nowadays a luxury. Fortunately long standing traditions are maintained in the cooking of game birds and there are some very tasty preparations.

Chicken de Vaux

*From **The Open Arms** in Dirleton, East Lothian, Scotland.*

Serves 4

4 boneless breasts of chicken
30 g (1 oz) onions, minced
30 g (1 oz) button mushrooms, minced
seasoned flour
egg wash (1 egg yolk mixed with a little cold water)

1½ cups (6 oz) dry breadcrumbs
1 tablespoon vegetable oil
25 g (¾ oz) butter
2 cups (16 fl oz) brown sauce (see p. 139)
1½ tablespoons whisky

1. Make a small cut in the chicken breasts and stuff them with the mixed onions and mushrooms. Close the opening with toothpicks.
2. Coat the breasts with the seasoned flour, then dip them in the eggwash and then coat them with the breadcrumbs.
3. Heat the oil and butter in a frying pan and cook the chicken for 5 minutes on each side. Place the chicken on a serving dish.
4. Heat the brown sauce in a pan, add the whisky and pour it around the chicken breasts.
5. Garnish with tomatoes and asparagus tips.

Right: After the hunt, clockwise from bottom left: A colourful pheasant cock, guinea fowl, quail, a pheasant hen and a duck.

Hindle Wakes Chicken

*From the **Waterside Restaurant** in Romiley, Manchester.*
This dish was brought to England by Flemish spinners in the 12th century. It was served during the annual Wakes Week near Bolton where the spinners settled.

Serves 4-6

1 large onion, finely chopped
1 cup (2 oz) soft breadcrumbs
2 cups (12 oz) stoned prunes, chopped
1 tablespoon grated suet
1 tablespoon mixed herbs
pinch mace and cinnamon
juice of 1 lemon
1 large boiling fowl
½ cup (4 fl oz) white wine vinegar
2 tablespoons brown sugar

Sauce
30 g (1 oz) butter
¼ cup (1 oz) flour
¼ cup (2 fl oz) milk
juice and rind of 1 lemon
⅔ cup (5 fl oz) cream
⅔ cup (5 fl oz) stock from chicken
Garnish
12 prunes, stoned, halved and soaked in water
1 lemon, thinly sliced
grated lemon rind
parsley

1. Mix together the onion, breadcrumbs, prunes, suet, herbs, spices, and lemon juice and stuff the bird with it.
2. Put it into a large pot and cover with water into which you have mixed the vinegar and brown sugar.
3. Cover the pan and simmer for 2½-3 hours or until the fowl is tender.
4. Leave the bird to cool in the stock.
5. Drain it, skin it and place it on a serving dish.
6. To make the sauce, melt the butter, stir in the flour and cook, stirring constantly for 2 minutes then add the milk.
7. Stir well, add the degreased chicken stock and simmer for 5 minutes. Season, add the lemon juice and rind and the cream.
8. Simmer for 5 minutes, then leave to cool.
9. Coat the chicken with the sauce, sprinkle with grated lemon rind and decorate with prunes, lemon slices and parsley. Serve cold.

Cyw Iar Mewn Mel

Chicken in Honey

*From the **King's Head Hotel** in Monmouth, Wales.*

Serves 4

1 large roasting chicken
3 tablespoons honey
3 tablespoons English mustard

1 cup (4 oz) dry breadcrumbs
oil for deep frying

1. Poach the chicken for 45 minutes, remove, and when cool enough to handle, skin it and cut it into joints.
2. Mix together the honey and mustard and coat each piece of chicken with it.
3. Roll the chicken pieces in breadcrumbs and leave in the fridge for 30 minutes.
4. Heat the deep frying oil and fry the chicken pieces for 7-10 minutes or until golden brown.
5. Serve with apple rings fried in butter.

Devonshire Chicken Dumplings

Serves 4-6

250 g (8 oz) cooked chicken meat
2 fried chicken livers
2 fried slices of bacon
2 cups (8 oz) dried breadcrumbs
2 eggs, lightly beaten
salt and pepper
2 sprigs parsley, finely chopped

flour
3-4 cups (24 fl oz-1 litre) chicken
stock (see p. 138)
2 egg yolks, lightly beaten
⅔ cup (5 fl oz) cream
½ cup (2 oz) grated cheese
finely chopped parsley for garnish

1. Mince the chicken meat, livers and bacon together and mix it with breadcrumbs, eggs, salt, pepper and parsley.
2. Roll the mixture into balls the size of walnuts and sprinkle them with flour.
3. Over low heat simmer them in chicken stock for 12 to 15 minutes.
4. Remove them to an ovenproof dish and keep them warm.
5. To make the sauce, combine the egg yolks, cream and 1¼ cups (10 fl oz) of the cooking liquid. Season to taste and simmer over low heat without boiling.
6. Pour the sauce over the dumplings, sprinkle with cheese and brown under a hot grill. Serve hot, sprinkled with parsley.

Chicken Casserole with Potatoes and Onions

Serves 4

1.3 kg (2 lb 10 oz) chicken,
cut into 4 portions
flour
30 g (1 oz) butter
2 onions, sliced

500 g (1 lb) peeled, sliced potatoes
salt and freshly ground pepper
2 cups (16 fl oz) hot chicken stock
(see p. 138) or water
¼ cup (1 oz) grated cheese
chopped parsley

1. Preheat oven to 180°C (350°F /Gas 4).
2. Dust the chicken pieces with flour and fry in butter until light brown.
3. Place a layer of onions and potatoes in a casserole and sprinkle them lightly with salt and pepper.
4. Put the chicken pieces on top and cover them with the remaining potatoes and onions, season.
5. Add the hot stock, or water, cover with a lid and cook in the oven for 1 hour.
6. Turn the heat up to 200°C (400°F /Gas 6), sprinkle the top with cheese and return to the oven, uncovered, for 30 minutes or until the top is brown. Serve hot sprinkled with parsley.

Roast Borrowdale Duckling with Bilberry and Apple Sauce

*This recipe comes from **The Pheasant Inn** on Bassenthwaite Lake in Cumberland.*
The building which houses The Pheasant Inn dates back to the 16th century and it is what a country pub ought to look like: whitewashed walls with black trim. Inside there are low cosy rooms with beamed ceilings and a particularly pleasant old worldly, tobacco smoke-stained bar.
The food prepared by the Pheasant Inn was local country fare: potted Silloth shrimps, highly spiced Cumberland sausages with apple sauce, roast Borrowdale duckling with bilberry and apple sauce and for dessert Peil Wyke raspberry syllabub.

Serves 4

2-2.5 kg (4-5 lb) oven ready duckling
¼ cup (3 oz) honey
salt and black pepper
Sauce
3 cooking apples, peeled, cored and diced
30 g (1 oz) butter
¾ cup (6 oz) sugar

250 g (8 oz) bilberries (or substitute cranberries)
juice of 1 lemon
salt and black pepper
1 tablespoon soy sauce
1 teaspoon Worcestershire sauce
⅓ cup (2½ fl oz) water
3 tablespoons cornflour (cornstarch)

1. Preheat the oven to 190°C (375°F/Gas 5).
2. Truss the duckling and place it on a rack in a roasting dish.
3. Season it with salt and pepper and spread the breast liberally with honey.
4. Bake for 1 hour or until cooked.

Sauce
1. Place the apples, butter and sugar in a pan and cook until very soft.
2. Add the bilberries and lemon juice and continue cooking for 5 minutes.
3. Add pepper and salt, soy sauce, Worcestershire sauce and water and bring to the boil.
4. Mix the cornflour to a paste with a little water and add it to the sauce mixture. Stir until sauce is thick, then serve with the duck.

Right: A fine display of Cornish dishes. Clockwise from bottom left: Cornish Pasties (see p. 72), Cornish Roast Lobster (see p. 36), Grandmother's Birthday Cake (see p. 82), Saffron Cake (see p. 93), Stargazy Pie (see p. 77), Squab Pie (see p. 77), Smoked Mackerel.

Coachmakers Arms, Callington, Cornwall

The coachmakers have long departed but the Coachmakers Arms still retains the appearance and air of days gone by. Today the locals, as well as the traveller, enjoy Cornish hospitality and Cornish food. Roast lobster is Cornish fare, a local product freshly brought in by fishermen from the nearby shores.

The Stargazy Pie offered here has an interesting origin. It was made in a deep pie dish, the fish were stood up on their tails and pieces of potatoes, herbs and bacon were placed in between. Cream was added and the whole dish was covered with a pastry lid. The pastry was pushed down over the heads so that they protruded over the crust. It is said that there was no point in covering the inedible heads yet they added greatly to the flavour of the dish.

Cornish pasties originated as a miner's lunch, with the ingredients 'wrapped' in pastry. To make sure there was no confusion, the initials of the owner were marked on the corner of the pasty. Those offered at the Coachmakers Arms were delicious and I was told that the list of traditional fillings is very long: onions, mushrooms and potatoes; herbs, rabbit or chicken with potatoes and onions; lamb, turnips and onions; ham or bacon with onions and potatoes; even jam or apples.

Mwyaden Hallt Gymreig

Welsh Salted Duck

*From the **King's Head Hotel** in Monmouth, Wales.*
This dish is a typical Welsh speciality. The process of salting the duck for several days gives the bird a particular flavour much appreciated in Wales.

Serves 3-4

1 duck, weighing 1.5-2 kg (3-4 lb)
1 onion
1 teaspoon finely chopped fresh sage
1 teaspoon sea salt

Sauce
2½ cups (20 fl oz) Béchamel sauce
  (see p. 140)
1 onion, finely chopped
salt and pepper

1. Preheat the oven to 190°C (375°F/Gas 5).
2. Stuff the duck with the whole onion. Sprinkle sage and salt all over the skin, pressing down well.
3. Roast the duck for about 1½ hours, depending upon its size (allow 20 minutes per 500 g plus an extra 20 minutes).
4. Remove the onion from the duck and purée it in a blender. Add it to the hot Béchamel sauce along with the chopped raw onion, salt and pepper. Cook for 5 minutes.
5. Cut the duck into portions and serve decorated with watercress. Serve the sauce separately.

Duckling in Honey Sauce

Serves 4

100 g (3½ oz) butter
2 small ducklings (about 1.2 kg/2 lb
  6 oz each)
½ cup (4 fl oz) dry white wine
salt, freshly ground black pepper
2 onions, finely chopped

¼ cup (2 fl oz) honey
2 sprigs thyme, finely chopped
juice of ½ lemon
1¼ cup (10 fl oz) cream
3 sprigs parsley, finely chopped

1. Preheat oven to 180°C (350°F/Gas 4).
2. Melt half of the butter in an ovenproof dish and sauté the duckling until light brown all round.
3. Add the wine, salt and pepper, tightly cover with foil and place it in the preheated oven for 1½ hours or until cooked.
4. In a large frying pan melt the rest of the butter and slowly sauté the onions until light golden brown.
5. Skim the surplus fat from the duck cooking liquid and add the liquid to the onions.
6. Mix in the honey, thyme, lemon juice, cream, season to taste and cook for 5 minutes.
7. Split each duckling lengthwise into two.
8. Place the duckling halves on a preheated serving platter and strain the hot sauce over them. Serve sprinkled with parsley.

Stuffed Boiled Turkey with Celery Sauce

Serves 6

1 small turkey (about 3 kg/6 lb)
250 g (8 oz) minced veal and pork
100 g (3⅓ oz) dried apricots,
   soaked overnight and finely chopped
125 g (4 oz) ham, finely chopped
2 cups (4 oz) fresh breadcrumbs
4 sprigs parsley, chopped
juice of 1 lemon
salt and freshly ground pepper

1 egg, lightly beaten
4 sprigs of fresh herbs, bound together
1 onion, studded with 6 cloves
4 stalks celery, cut into 2 cm (1 inch)
   lengths
2 carrots, chopped
6 peppercorns
2 bay leaves
30 g (1 oz) butter
¼ cup (1 oz) flour

1. To make the stuffing, mix together well the minced meat, apricots, ham, breadcrumbs, parsley, lemon juice, salt, pepper and egg.
2. Stuff the turkey and secure the opening.
3. Place the turkey in a large saucepan, add the herbs, onion, celery, carrots, peppercorns, bay leaves and salt.
4. Cover with water, bring slowly to the boil and skim if necessary.
5. Cover and simmer over low heat for approximately 1½ hours or until the turkey is tender.
6. Remove the turkey from the liquid and keep it warm.
7. To make the sauce, strain and save the cooking liquid. Take out the celery and rub it through a sieve, reserve the purée.
8. Melt the butter, add the flour and without browning, cook for 2 minutes, add 2½ cups (20 fl oz) of the hot cooking liquid and mix to a smooth sauce.
9. Add the celery purée, season to taste and cook for 3 to 4 minutes.
10. Carve the turkey and arrange the meat and stuffing on a preheated serving plate. Garnish with sprigs of parsley.
11. Rub the sauce through a sieve and serve it separately in a sauce boat.

Pheasant in Cider

Serves 4

60 g (2 oz) butter
2 small pheasants
juice of 1 lemon
2 sprigs rosemary, finely chopped
2 sprigs thyme, finely chopped
salt and freshly ground pepper

3 cooking apples, peeled, cored and sliced
½ teaspoon cinnamon
1 cup (8 fl oz) cider
¼ cup (2 fl oz) cream
finely chopped parsley for garnish

1. Preheat oven to 180°C (350°F/Gas 4).
2. In a casserole melt half of the butter and brown the pheasants all round.
3. Remove the pheasants from the casserole and sprinkle the insides with lemon juice, rosemary, thyme, salt and pepper.
4. Melt the rest of the butter and lightly sauté the apples.
5. Return the pheasants to the casserole and pour a mixture of cinnamon, cider and cream over them.
6. Cover the casserole and put it in the preheated oven for 50 to 60 minutes or until the pheasants are cooked.
7. Season to taste, split the pheasants into two, lengthwise, place them on a heated serving platter. Arrange the apples round them, pour the sauce over the birds and serve sprinkled with parsley.

Chequers Inn, Fowlmere, Near Royston

Host, James Holditch, and his chefs, take great pride in serving traditional English food. Potted duck and prawn mousse make a good starter to a meal of pork, baked in pastry and served with apricot sauce.

Chicken in a lavender sauce has the fragrance of an English herb garden.

To satisfy the English liking for rich desserts, they offer Chocolate Raisin and Rum Cheesecake and, for those who prefer something lighter, there is Iced Melon Sorbet.

The restaurant has an intimate and warm feeling, and the many guests who come to taste the food are assured of an enjoyable evening.

Right: Clockwise from bottom left: Potted Duck (see p. 16), Fillet of Pork in pastry, Prawn Mousse, Chicken in a Lavender Sauce, Chocolate Raisin and Rum Cheesecake.

Guinea Fowl with Tudor Sauce

*From **The Bell Inn**, Long Hanborough, Oxfordshire.*

Serves 6

3 guinea fowl
45 g (1½ oz) butter
2 large onions, finely chopped
125 g (4 oz) mushrooms, finely chopped

2 tablespoons flour
1¼ cups (10 fl oz) dry red wine
salt and freshly ground pepper

1. Preheat oven to 200°C (400°F/Gas 6).
2. Place the guinea fowl and one-third of the butter in the preheated oven and cook for 30 minutes, basting occasionally with the butter. Reduce the heat to 150°C (300°F/Gas 2) and cook until tender.
3. Melt the remaining butter and sauté the onions until soft, add the mushrooms and cook for 5 minutes.
4. Add the flour, cook for 3 to 4 minutes, add the wine and stir well. Season and cook the sauce for 5 to 8 minutes.
5. Rub the sauce through a sieve.
6. Split the birds into two, lengthwise, and serve with the sauce poured over.

Pigeon and Prune Compote

*From the **Hunters Lodge Restaurant**, Broadway, Worcestershire.*

Serves 4

4 pigeons
¾ cup (6 fl oz) dry red wine
⅓ cup (2 fl oz) wine vinegar
6 crushed juniper berries
60 g (2 oz) butter
salt and freshly ground pepper

60 g (2 oz) bacon, diced
12 peeled, small pickling-type onions
6 teaspoons (½ oz) flour
2 carrots, peeled and diced
16 prunes, stoned

1. With a sharp knife remove the legs and breasts from the pigeons.
2. Place the carcasses in a saucepan, add the wine, vinegar, juniper berries and enough water to cover.
3. Cover with a lid, bring to the boil and simmer over low heat for 40 minutes.
4. Melt the butter in a frying pan, season the pigeon pieces and lightly fry them until golden brown. Place them in a saucepan.
5. In the frying pan in the remaining butter, fry the bacon and onions, take them out and add them to the pigeons.
6. Sprinkle the flour into the frying pan and cook for a few minutes to make a light brown roux.
7. Strain enough pigeon stock into the roux to make a light sauce.
8. Strain the sauce over the pigeon pieces.
9. Add the carrots and prunes, cover and simmer over very low heat for 50 minutes.
10. Season to taste and serve with mashed potatoes.

Thirlmere Forest Casserole of Venison

*This recipe comes from **Yan Tyan Tethera** in Keswick, Cumbria. These are the words still used by genuine Cumbrian shepherds to count sheep. It is an ancient local language which is similar to Welsh, Cornish and the language of Brittany.*

The restaurant is situated in a 16th century cottage, where classical music plays and the diner looks out over sunny surroundings. It's mostly 'international' food, but some Cumbrian dishes are served, e.g. Thirlmere Forest Casserole of Venison. I love the story about the origin of Cumberland Rum Butter, traditionally served at Christenings or, with whipped cream added, with Christmas Pudding.

The tale goes that a ship from the Cumbrian Coast had collected its cargo of spices, rum and sugar from the West Indies, called on Ireland for butter, and then came across a storm, which loosened the various barrels. The resultant mixture tasted so good it became a Cumbrian speciality.

Serves 4-6

Marinade	Casserole
1 onion, chopped	1.25 kg (2½ lb) venison
1 carrot, chopped	155 g (5 oz) streaky (fat) bacon,
½ stick celery, chopped	cut into strips
6 peppercorns	1 tablespoon olive oil
4 juniper berries, crushed	250 g (8 oz) onions, chopped
2 tablespoons olive oil	250 g (8 oz) carrots, chopped
red wine	250 g (8 oz) celery, chopped
	1 cup (4 oz) flour
	salt
	1-2 tablespoons redcurrant jelly

1. Place all the marinade ingredients except the wine in a large bowl, place the piece of venison on top and pour over enough red wine to cover the meat. Leave to marinate 24 hours, turning occasionally.
2. Remove the venison from the marinade, dry it well with paper towels and cut it into 2.5 cm (1 inch) cubes.
3. Heat the oil in a frying pan and add the bacon and venison. Fry on all sides to seal the meat.
4. Add the vegetables, then the flour, stirring well.
5. Add sufficient strained marinade to almost cover the meat and vegetables.
6. Simmer the liquid, stirring constantly, until it has thickened. Cover the pan and cook very slowly for 2 to 4 hours depending upon the age of the meat. Test after 2 hours — the meat should not be chewy, but it must not fall apart either.
7. Add the redcurrant jelly to taste.
8. Traditionally this is served with jacket potatoes and red cabbage.

MEAT AND GAME

The English have the well-founded reputation for being a race of meat eaters, especially of beef. Roast beef is Britain's national dish.

It has been the staple food of the noble and rich, and the frequently unfulfilled dream of peasants and the poor, who for centuries subsisted on salted bacon and game poached in defiance of severe punishment. The amount of meat eaten was, in those days, an indication of one's prosperity. The poor had to make do with what happened to be available and so were responsible for the development of dishes with vegetables, dried pulses or seafood.

Today good quality meat in Britain is readily available and within everybody's reach. There are many tasty and filling stews and pies in the regional cooking of most countries: the pickled stew of Scotland, spiced beef from Wales and Lancashire hot-pot.

Good pork is available throughout the country and traditional pork dishes can be found in England and Wales. The English are justifiably proud of their roast pork and nowhere have I eaten better crisp and crunchy crackling than in Britain. Cider, beer, apples, apricots and other fruit form part of the most popular dishes.

Until about two hundred years ago, sheep were mainly bred for their wool and lamb was hardly ever eaten. Only older, unproductive animals found their way into the stewpot. In more recent time, lamb has become plentiful and popular. In the Devon Lamb Stew (see p. 64), three regional products: prime lamb, cider and cream combine to create a truly local dish.

In the past, game was very much part of the nobleman's table, but with the growth of human settlement, intensive agriculture and the spread of industry, the hunting grounds have greatly diminished. Now considered a luxury, what little game is available is prepared in accordance with long established traditional recipes.

The Fox at Ansty near Bulbarrow in the heart of Dorset

I had heard about English country lanes but never had any experience of them. With both sides of the camping van touching the hedges, and visibility to the next corner a few yards away, it was a hair-raising experience.

The journey to Ansty was well worthwhile as at the end of the short if nerve-wracking journey I was met with warm hospitality by my landlords Peter and Wendy Amey. Their Fox Inn is a delightful Victorian Wessex flint and brick house where they welcome locals and travellers to a most unusual ''feast''.

In the Toby Bar where they display one of the largest collections of jugs in the country, they offer a great choice of delicious cold meats, such as stuffed legs of pork and beef topside. There are pies and Dorset pâté, roast pheasant, guinea fowl, duckling and turkey. There is also the choice of some thirty salads. Their ''sweets'' are delicious and if at the end of such a generous meal there is room, almond meringue and Martini gâteau are offered, along with others.

The Hall and Woodhouse, one of the few remaining independent brewers in England, started here and the Fox takes pride in serving very fine 'real' ale and one of the world's strongest beers.

The Dorset countryside is very tranquil and beautiful and there are some excellent bridleways. Hunting with the South Dorset Hunt, if you like that sort of thing, sounds like fun.

Right: The rich display of cold meats, pâtés, terrines and salads offered to the hungry traveller at the Fox at Ansty.

Roast Beef

*As prepared by the chef at the **Black Bull Inn**, Moulton, Richmond, Yorkshire, the timing and the temperatures are rather unusual but since I have partaken of the dinner at which it was served, I can vouch for its excellence. As much higher temperatures are required for the Yorkshire Pudding, it has to be cooked separately.*

9 kg (18 lb) rib roast at room temperature

1. Preheat the oven to 150°C (300°F/Gas 2).
2. Place the roast on top of a rack, fat side up.
3. Roast it for 4 hours, then reduce the heat to 70°C (160°F) and cook it for 1 hour more.
4. Remove the roast from the oven and let it stand for 15 minutes before carving.
5. Serve with its cooking juices, Yorkshire Pudding and horseradish.

Note: If cooking smaller quantities, allow approximately 375 g (12 oz) gross weight of meat and bones per person. Cook in a 240°C (475°F/Gas 9) oven for the first 30 minutes, then reduce temperature to 180°C (350°F/Gas 4) and roast for a further hour. Use a meat thermometer 60°C (140°F) for rare, 60°-70°C (149°-150°F) for medium and 75°C (167°F) for well done.

Yorkshire Pudding

500 g (1 lb) flour
pinch of salt and pepper
4 eggs

2½ cups (20 fl oz) milk
1¼ cups (10 fl oz) water
dripping

1. Preheat oven to 230°C (450°F/Gas 8).
2. Mix the flour, salt and pepper together.
3. Make a well in the middle, add the eggs and gradually the milk and water to make a batter.
4. Allow the batter to stand for an hour before use.
5. Heat the dripping in a mould until very hot, pour in the batter.
6. Cook in the preheated oven until it has risen then lower the temperature to 180°C (350°F/Gas 4) and cook for 40 to 45 minutes.

Marinated Beef Stew

Serves 4

¼ cup (2 fl oz) cider vinegar
¼ cup (2 fl oz) olive oil
16 peppercorns
2 bay leaves
2 cloves
2 sprigs parsley, chopped
1 sprig thyme, chopped

3 onions, sliced
1 sprig marjoram, chopped
   or ½ teaspoon dry marjoram
750 g (1½ lb) shin beef, cut into
   4 pieces
30 g (1 oz) dripping
1½ cups (12 fl oz) beef stock (see
   p. 138)
1-2 tablespoons cornflour (cornstarch)

1. To make the marinade, mix together the vinegar, oil, peppercorns, bay leaves, cloves, parsley, thyme, onions and marjoram.
2. Place the meat in a dish and pour the marinade over it. Marinate for 12 hours turning the meat several times.
3. Dry the meat, melt the dripping in a casserole and brown it all round.
4. Add the stock and strained marinade, cover and simmer over low heat for 45 to 60 minutes or until the meat is tender.
5. Season to taste and thicken the sauce with cornflour. Serve hot with boiled potatoes.

Braised Beef with Anchovies

Serves 4

6 anchovy fillets
30 g (1 oz) butter
750 g (1½ lb) topside beef
2 onions, roughly chopped
1 leek, sliced
2 carrots, sliced

3 stalks celery, sliced
6 peppercorns
2 bay leaves
3 sprigs fresh herbs, chopped
1¾ cups (14 fl oz) beef stock (see
   p. 138)
salt (optional)

1. Mash three anchovies with half of the butter, melt it in a casserole and brown the meat on all sides.
2. Take the meat out, melt the rest of the butter, add the vegetables and sauté them for 5 to 8 minutes.
3. Add the peppercorns, bay leaves, herbs and stock. Place the meat on top, cover the casserole with a lid and braise over very low heat for 2½ hours.
4. Season to taste being careful with the salt as the anchovies may be sufficient.
5. To serve, carve the meat into slices and arrange them on a heated serving plate garnished with the remaining anchovies. You may serve it with the vegetables and cooking liquid or you can strain the liquid, thicken it with flour and serve the sauce with the meat.

Glantraeth Tournedos

*From **The Chequers** in Mold, Clwyd, Wales.*

Serves 4

4-250 g (8 oz) fillet steaks
250 g (8 oz) country-style pâté
seasoned flour
1 egg, beaten
1 cup (5 oz) rolled oats

½ cup (4 fl oz) vegetable oil
¼ cup (2 fl oz) dry sherry
½ cup (4 fl oz) cream
salt and pepper

1. Make an incision along one side of each steak right through to the centre.
2. Fill this cavity with the pâté.
3. Roll the steaks in flour, then egg then rolled oats.
4. Heat the oil in a frying pan and fry the steaks on both sides until well browned.
5. Preheat the oven to 180°C (350°F/Gas 4).
6. Transfer the steaks to a baking dish and bake for 8 to 10 minutes.
7. Add the sherry to the frying pan and with a wooden spoon scrape up all the brown bits clinging to the pan. Add the cream and heat gently.
8. Pour the sauce over the steaks and serve.

Venison, Beefsteak and Mushroom Casserole

*From the **Bell Inn**, Long Hanborough, Oxfordshire.*

Serves 6

750 g (1½ lb) venison,
** cut into 1.25 cm (½ inch) dice**
750 g (1½ lb) beef,
** cut into 1.25 cm (½ inch) dice**
60 g (2 oz) lard
2 large onions, chopped

2 tablespoons flour
1¼ cups (10 fl oz) redcurrant wine
** or any sweet red wine**
250 g (8 oz) mushrooms, sliced
salt and freshly ground pepper

1. Preheat the oven to 150°C (300°F/Gas 2).
2. Sauté the venison and beef in the lard until brown. Remove from the pan.
3. Add the onions to the remaining fat and sauté until soft.
4. Add the flour and cook for 2 to 3 minutes.
5. Add the wine and stir until smooth. Cook for 2 to 3 minutes.
6. Transfer the meat, onions and sauce to a casserole, add mushrooms and season to taste.
7. Cover the casserole and cook in the oven for 2½ to 3 hours or until meat is tender.

Right: The typical and traditional architecture of Chester.

English Oxtail with Dumplings

*From the **Cavendish Hotel**, Baslow, Bakewell, Derbyshire.*
The Cavendish Hotel has a very tasteful interior and could certainly be a home away from home for many of its guests.
From the outside it looks like an opulent manor house and commands a view over the gentle, undulating Derbyshire landscape.
Among the food they serve there is Chatsworth venison named after the nearby Chatsworth House, the ancestral home of the Dukes of Devonshire. It is indeed an aristocratic dish, and contrasts well with the farmer's rabbit pie and the local bakewell pudding.

Serves 8

4 oxtails cut into pieces
seasoned flour
30 g (1 oz) dry English mustard
125 g (4 oz) onions, chopped
125 g (4 oz) mushrooms, chopped
2 bay leaves
125 g (4 oz) carrots
salt, freshly ground pepper
1¼ cups (10 fl oz) dry red wine
Brown Sauce
4 onions, chopped
90 g (3 oz) dripping

5 tablespoons flour
5 cups (1.25 litres) beef stock
  (see p. 138) or water
3 tablespoons Worcestershire sauce
3 tablespoons vinegar
Dumplings
125 g (4 oz) suet
500 g (1 lb) flour
1 tablespoon baking powder
salt and pepper
water
chopped parsley for garnish

1. Soak the oxtail for 24 hours in cold water.
2. Dry and roll in a mixture of seasoned flour and mustard.
3. Place it in a dry stewpan and fry. The oxtail will render its own fat.
4. Add the onions, mushrooms, bay leaves, carrots, salt and pepper and sauté lightly.
5. Add the wine and brown sauce.
6. Cover the pan, cook the oxtail for 2½ hours or until meat is tender and falls off the bones.
7. Garnish with parsley and serve with dumplings, broad beans and boiled new potatoes.

Brown Sauce
Sauté the onions in the dripping until they are browned. Drain off fat. Add the flour and cook until it browns. Add the stock or water and stir until it boils. Add the Worcestershire sauce and vinegar and simmer for 10 minutes. Strain.
Dumplings
Mix together the suet, flour, baking powder, salt and pepper, add enough water to make firm soft dough. Roll into 16 small balls and simmer in a pan of salted water for about 30 minutes.

Toad-in-the-Hole

A homely dish, using meat leftovers. Today the Yorkshire Pudding batter is poured over slices of sausage but originally any leftover meat was used.
*This recipe, from the **Cavendish Hotel**, in Baslow, Derbyshire, is a rather more sophisticated version.*

Makes four 12.5 cm (5 inch) puddings

500 g (1 lb) rump steak, cubed
125 g (4 oz) kidney, chopped
1 onion, chopped
60 g (2 oz) mushrooms, chopped
60 g (2 oz) butter
3 tablespoons plain flour
⅔ cup (5 fl oz) dry red wine
salt and freshly ground pepper

Yorkshire Pudding Batter
1½ cups (6 oz) flour
3 eggs
1¼ cups (10 fl oz) milk
dripping

1. To make the filling fry the meat, kidney, onion, and mushrooms in the butter until golden brown.
2. Sprinkle with flour, add the wine and if necessary, some water to make a sauce. Season to taste.
3. Simmer over low heat for 30 to 40 minutes or until the liquid has reduced by half.
4. To make Yorkshire puddings, beat the flour, eggs and some of the milk to make a paste, season and add the rest of the milk.
5. Rest the batter for 2 hours.
6. Preheat the oven to 200°C (400°F/Gas 6).
7. Preheat the pudding dishes, add some dripping, divide the batter into four and pour it into the dishes.
8. Place them into the preheated oven and bake for approximately 35 to 45 minutes. The puddings will rise at the sides leaving a well in the centre.
9. To serve take the puddings out of the dishes and fill them with the meat mixture.

Spiced Beef

*From the **George Hotel**, Chollerford, Northumberland.*

Serves 6-8

1 teaspoon salt
1 teaspoon sugar
1 teaspoon allspice
10 peppercorns

10 cloves
2 kg (4 lb) brisket or leg of beef
250 g (8 oz) fat or lard
2½ cups (20 fl oz) water

1. Mix together the salt, sugar, allspice, peppercorns and cloves and place them on a large dish.
2. Roll the meat in them, cover with foil and refrigerate for three days, turning it in the spices every day.
3. On the fourth day, wash the meat, dry it well and tie it into a roll.
4. Heat the fat in a pan until it is smoking and add the meat. Seal it on all sides then add the water and simmer for 3 to 4 hours, or until it is tender.
5. Remove the meat from the pan and place it in a mould. Cover with a heavily weighted plate and leave to cool.
6. Serve with salad.

Beef Olives

Serves 4

125 g (4 oz) veal, minced
60 g (2 oz) ham, finely chopped
½ cup (1 oz) fresh breadcrumbs
2 sprigs parsley, chopped
salt and freshly ground pepper
1 egg, lightly beaten

500 g (1 lb) rump steak, cut into
  4 thin slices and lightly beaten
30 g (1 oz) butter
2 onions, sliced
1¾ cups (14 fl oz) beef stock (see
  p. 380)
½ cup (4 fl oz) dry red wine
1 tablespoon tomato purée

1. To make the stuffing, mix together the veal, ham, breadcrumbs, parsley, salt, pepper and egg.
2. Divide it into 4 parts and spread it on the steak slices.
3. Roll them up and tie them with thread or string. These are known as *olives*.
4. In a casserole, melt the butter and sauté the onions. Add the olives and lightly brown them.
5. Add the stock, wine, tomato purée and season to taste.
6. Cover the casserole and simmer over very low heat for 1½ hours.
7. To serve, arrange the olives on a heated platter. The sauce may be thickened with flour and strained over the meat.

Reform Club Cutlets

*A dish created in the 19th century by Alexis Soyer renowned chef at the **Reform Club** in London.*

Serves 6

12 lamb cutlets
  approximately 100 g (3⅓ oz) each
flour seasoned with salt and pepper
2 eggs, lightly beaten
15 g (½ oz) finely chopped ham
15 g (½ oz) finely chopped, cooked
  tongue
2 sprigs parsley, finely chopped
2 cups (8 oz) dry breadcrumbs

oil for frying
Garnish
30 g (1 oz) each of chopped ham,
  tongue and gherkins, hardboiled egg
  white, cooked beetroot and truffles
  (optional)
125 g (4 oz) butter
2½ cups (20 fl oz) Reform Club sauce
  (see p. 140)

1. Trim off the fat and slightly flatten the cutlets.
2. Dust them with seasoned flour, dip them in egg and heavily coat them in a mixture of ham, tongue, parsley and breadcrumbs.
3. Fry them in hot oil on both sides until cooked and golden brown.
4. To serve arrange them on a serving platter.
5. Toss the garnish inredients in some of the butter and arrange them around the cutlets.
6. Melt the rest of the butter, fry it until it is light brown and pour it over the cutlets. Serve the sauce separately in a sauce boat.

Right: The rich bounty of the land offered at Invereshie House, bottom left from the hunter's bag: wild pigeon, pheasant, hare, grouse and wild duck. From the pantry: smoked salmon, Our Game Pie (see p. 76), fresh salmon, lobster, Arbroath Smokies, Highland Mist, Murray Forth prawns and Crowdie Cheesecake.

Invereshie House, Kincraig, Scotland

My visit to Invereshie House turned out to be one of the highlights of my gastronomic journey through Britain.

Frances and Allan Hobkirk are most charming hosts and it is my regret that I could not stay longer.

Invereshie House, a 17th Century Highland Shooting lodge, is situated at the foot of the Cairngorm mountains right in the middle of some of the best skiing country in Scotland. It also has some 75,000 acres of shooting right and attracts hunters from all over the world.

Stalking red deer, shooting blackgame grouse, pheasant, partridge and blue mountain hare, together with fishing for salmon and trout in the river and loch Insh, make it one of the finest sporting places in Scotland.

The Hobkirks have a very open approach to cooking and with such rich bounty at their disposal how can they fail? The recipe for grouse stuffed with Haggis starts with the following words: "We only use young grouse. Mr Hamlett of Kingussie makes our Haggis – good and savoury." And they conclude: "Some Highland recipes suggest you pour a dram of whisky over the birds – but that is a waste of good whisky. Just serve the Whisky separately!!" "Our Game Pie" contains venison, 4 whole pigeons or 6 whole quail.

Crown of Lamb

*From the **George Hotel**, Chollerford, Northumberland.*

Serves 6

1 crown of lamb of 12 ribs
1 cup (8 fl oz) port
60 g (2 oz) tomato purée

1 cup (4 oz) flour
2½ cups (20 fl oz) chicken stock
 (see p. 138)
pepper and salt

1. Preheat the oven to 180°C (350°F /Gas 4).
2. Trim the lamb if the butcher hasn't already done so and cover the bones with foil.
3. Roast for 45 minutes, then remove it from the oven and keep it warm while you make the gravy.
4. Skim the fat from the pan juices and stir in the flour.
5. Put the roasting tin over a high heat and stir well until the flour has browned. Add the tomato purée, port, stock, pepper and salt, bring to the boil, stirring constantly and simmer for 3 to 4 minutes until the gravy is smooth.
6. Place cutlet frills on the lamb bones and serve it with vegetables, redcurrant jelly and the gravy.

Devon Lamb Stew

Serves 4

8 lamb chops trimmed of all fat
30 g (1 oz) butter
400 g (12½ oz) small potatoes, peeled
10 small pickling-type onions
16 button mushrooms
½ cup (4 fl oz) hard cider (alcoholic)

1 cup (8 fl oz) beef stock (see p. 138)
½ cup (4 fl oz) cream
salt and freshly ground pepper
2 bay leaves
2 sprigs thyme, chopped
4 sprigs parsley, finely chopped

1. In a casserole brown the chops in the butter.
2. Remove the meat and lightly brown the potatoes, onions and mushrooms.
3. Drain off excess fat.
4. Add the cider, stock, cream, salt, pepper, bay leaves, thyme, half the parsley and mix thoroughly.
5. Return the meat to the dish, cover and simmer over low heat for 1 hour or until the meat is tender. Serve garnished with the rest of the parsley.

Elizabethan Stewed Pork

Serves 6

1 kg (2 lb) boneless shoulder of pork
2 tablespoons cooking oil
3 onions, sliced
2 cooking apples, peeled,
    quartered and sliced
salt and freshly ground pepper
2 tablespoons flour
100 g (3⅓ oz) seedless grapes
    when in season or sultanas

6 seeded dates
1 sprig each parsley and sage, chopped
½ bunch of celery, chopped
1 orange, peeled, cut into eighths and
    pitted
1¼ cups (10 fl oz) dry red or white
    wine
beef stock (see p. 138) or water

1. Preheat the oven to 180°C (350°F/Gas 4).
2. In a casserole brown the meat in the hot oil.
3. Remove the meat and lightly sauté the onions.
4. Add the apple slices, salt and pepper.
5. Dust the meat with the flour and place it on top of the apples.
6. Add the grapes or sultanas, dates, parsley, sage, celery, orange peel cut into thin slivers and the orange.
7. Pour in the wine and add enough stock or water to cover the meat.
8. Cover the casserole and cook it in the preheated oven for 2 to 2½ hours or until meat is tender.
9. Remove the meat, carve it into slices and arrange them on a serving platter.
10. Strain the cooking liquid and rub the vegetables and fruit through the strainer.
11. If necessary, reduce the liquid to 1½ to 2 cups (12 to 16 fl oz) season and serve it from a sauce boat.

St Tudno's Pork

*From **The Chequers** in Mold, Clwyd, Wales.*

Serves 4

1½ cups (12 fl oz) Béchamel sauce
    (see p. 140)
2 large tomatoes, peeled and cut into
    quarters
1 cup (8 fl oz) fish stock (see p. 139)

125 g (4 oz) small cooked prawns
4 pork chops
pepper and salt

1. Heat the Béchamel sauce and add the quartered tomatoes. Cook for 10 minutes, mashing the tomatoes well.
2. Add the fish stock and cook for a further 10 minutes. Strain.
3. Put the sauce back into the washed out pan and add the prawns. Reheat just until the prawns are hot.
4. Grill the pork chops and when they are cooked pour the prawn sauce over them and serve.

Escalope of Pork Tantallon

*From **The Open Arms** in Dirleton, East Lothian, Scotland.*

Serves 4

4 pork escalopes, about 60 g (2 oz) each
egg wash (1 egg yolk mixed with a little cold water)
1½ cups (7 oz) fine oatmeal
1 tablespoon vegetable oil
30 g (1 oz) butter

4 chicken livers, chopped
1½ tablespoons whisky, warmed
2 cups (16 fl oz) brown sauce (see p. 139)
finely chopped fresh parsley

1. Put the pork into the eggwash and then the oatmeal.
2. Heat the oil and butter and sauté the pork for 8-10 minutes, turning once. Remove them from the pan and keep them warm in a low oven.
3. Put the livers into the same pan and cook them over high heat until just tender but still slightly pink inside.
4. Pour the warmed whisky over them and set it alight. Remove the livers.
5. Add brown sauce to the pan and bring to the boil.
6. Pour the sauce over the pork and livers and serve sprinkled with parsley.

Cumberland Sausage with Apple Sauce

*From **The Pheasant Inn** on Bassenthwaite Lake, Cumberland.*
Cumberland sausage is a highly spiced pork sausage traditionally made into very thick lengths of about 30.5 cm (12 inches).
It is normally cooked curled in a spiral and can be eaten at breakfast or as a substantial lunchtime snack when served with a thick apple sauce.

Apple Sauce
500 g (1 lb) cooking apples, peeled, cored and diced
1 quince (optional), peeled, cored and diced

30 g (1 oz) butter
30 g (1 oz) sugar (optional)
2 cloves

1. Put the apples and quince in a pan with the butter and a tablespoon of water. Add sugar to taste and the cloves.
2. Cover and simmer for 15 minutes or until the apples are soft.
3. Purée in a blender or processor or rub through a sieve.
4. Return the purée to the pan and reduce over low heat to the desired consistency.

The Cavendish Hotel, Baslow, Bakewell, Derbyshire.
The Cavendish Hotel has a very tasteful interior and could certainly be a home away from home for many of its guests.
From the outside it looks like an opulent manor house and commands a view over the gentle, undulating Derbyshire landscape.
Among the food they serve there is Chatsworth venison named after the nearby Chatsworth House, the ancestral home of the Dukes of Devonshire. It is indeed an aristocratic dish, and contrasts well with the farmer's rabbit pie and the local bakewell pudding.
Right: Clockwise from bottom left: Farmer's Rabbit Pie (see p. 72), Chicken and tarragon, Chatsworth Venison, English Oxtail with Dumplings (see p. 60), Toad in the Hole (see p. 61), trout, Bakewell Pudding (see p. 84), Edenson Pancakes (see p. 78).

Scrumpied Tenderloin of Pork

*From the **Bush Hotel** in Farnham, Surrey.*
'Scrumpy' means rough, homemade cider, which was originally used in this recipe. Today any type of cider can be used.

Serves 4

500 g (1 lb) pork fillet, thinly sliced	**salt**
flour	**pepper**
125 g (4 oz) butter	**1¼ cups (10 fl oz) cider**
1 small onion, finely chopped	**1 apple, peeled, cored and thinly sliced**
60 g button mushrooms, sliced	**1 tablespoon finely chopped parsley**

1. Beat the pork slices with a meat mallet and dredge them in flour.
2. Melt the butter in a frying pan and sauté the onion for a few minutes.
3. Add the pork and fry quickly on each side, then add the mushrooms, pepper and salt and cook a further minute or two.
4. Pour in the cider and cook for about 30 minutes or until the pork has cooked and the sauce has reduced to a creamy consistency.
5. Place the pork and its sauce on a heat-proof serving dish and lay the apple slices on top. Put the dish under a preheated hot grill for 1 minute to heat and slightly brown the apples.
6. Sprinkle the dish with chopped parsley and serve.

Cider Baked Pork Chops

*From **The Anglers' Rest**, Fingle Bridge, Exeter.*

Serves 5

250 g (8 oz) cooking apples, peeled, cored and sliced	**5 pork chops**
1 large onion, sliced	**1¼ cups (10 fl oz) cider**
125 g (4 oz) mushrooms, sliced	**1 cup (4 oz) grated Cheddar cheese**
salt	**½ cup (2 oz) browned breadcrumbs**
pepper	**watercress for garnishing**

1. Preheat the oven to 200°C (400°F /Gas 6).
2. Grease a shallow baking dish.
3. Place the apples, onion and mushrooms on the bottom of the dish and sprinkle with salt and pepper.
4. Lay the pork chops on top and pour over the cider.
5. Mix together the cheese and breadcrumbs and sprinkle it over the chops.
6. Bake, uncovered, for 1¼ to 1½ hours or until the chops are cooked through.
7. Serve, garnished with watercress.

Baked Gammon with Cumberland Sauce

*From the **Parkend Restaurant** in Wigton, Cumbria.*
Cumberland Sauce derives its name from Ernest, Duke of Cumberland. It is most often served with game, ham and poultry.

Serves 8

piece of corner or middle gammon weighing 2.5 kg (5 lb), soaked overnight in cold water
1¼ cups (10 fl oz) cider
cloves
Glaze
4 tablespoons dark brown sugar
1 teaspoon dry mustard
pinch of mace
grated rind and juice of 1 orange

Cumberland Sauce
juice and rind of 2 oranges or 1 orange and 1 lemon
4 tablespoons redcurrant jelly
1 teaspoon dry mustard
½ cup (4 fl oz) port or red wine
salt and black pepper
pinch ground ginger

1. Drain the gammon and put it into a large pot. Cover with fresh cold water, bring to the boil and simmer for 1 hour. Preheat the oven to 180°C (350°F/Gas 4).
2. Remove the gammon from the pan, wipe it dry, wrap it loosely in foil, put it in a baking tin and bake for 45 minutes.
3. Remove the gammon from the oven and carefully lift off the skin. (To do this, lift the corner of the skin with a knife and pull the skin off with your fingers. If the joint is cooked, it should come away easily.)
4. Score the fat in a diamond pattern with a sharp knife.
5. Mix together all the glaze ingredients.
6. Spread this mixture over the fat, stud with cloves, pour the cider around it and return it to the oven for a further 20 minutes, basting occasionally with the cider, until the glaze is crisp and golden.
7. Serve hot or cold, garnish with watercress and fruit in season, e.g. slices of orange or pineapple or poached apricots and Cumberland Sauce.

Cumberland Sauce
1. Cut the fruit rind into fine matchsticks. Blanch for 5 minutes in boiling water then drain.
2. Heat the jelly and mustard together over low heat, stirring until smooth.
3. Add the fruit juice, wine, pepper, salt and ginger.
4. Stir in the peel and simmer for about 5 minutes, then pour into a sauce boat or glass bowl and serve cold.

Faggots

*From **Ty Mawr** in Brechfa, Wales.*

Serves 6

750 g (1½ lb) pig's liver
2 cups (4 oz) soft white breadcrumbs
90 g (3 oz) suet, grated
2 large onions, finely chopped

1 teaspoon chopped fresh sage
2 teaspoons salt
¼ teaspoon pepper

1. Mince the liver and add it to all the other ingredients in a bowl. Mix very well.
2. Preheat the oven to 190°C (375°F/Gas 5).
3. Form the mixture into small balls and place in one layer in a greased baking dish.
4. Bake for 30 minutes, then pour over 1¼ cups boiling water and cook for a further 10 minutes. (The water forms the gravy.) Serve at once.

PIES

In the days long before forks were introduced, the pie was a convenient way to eat meat and gravy with your fingers. Today, hundreds of years later, it still is.

Pies are an English invention and the name is said to have been derived from *magpie*, suggesting a collection of many things in the nest. In those days pies were a mixture of all sorts of ingredients.

Over the years eating tastes have changed a great deal. Until as recently as 200 years ago savoury and sweet ingredients were combined and meat was often sweetened. Pies were served at all festive occasions, even Royal banquets, and it is hard to imagine an English dinner without them.

Early examples were "raised" pies, like the still-popular cold pork pie of which the Melton Mowbray pie is the best known. These were made by forming the pastry casing around a jar or the outside of a pot. This process was called 'raising the coffin'.

At the end of the 19th century, thanks to the general acceptance of the potato, cottage or shepherd's pies started to become popular.

Puddings are of equally ancient origin. But instead of using a pastry crust, the ingredients were placed in the stomach bag of an animal. Today, except for the Scottish national dish, Haggis, cloth is used instead. The most frequently used method however is to steam the pudding in a pudding basin covered with a cloth or suet pastry.

Lancashire Steak Pie

*This recipe comes from the **Waterside Restaurant** in Romiley, Manchester.*

Serves 4

1 tablespoon vegetable oil	salt and pepper
1 large onion, finely chopped	1 tablespoon Worcestershire sauce
1 small stick celery, finely chopped	500 g (1 lb) short crust pastry
250 g (8 oz) minced beef	(see p. 141)
	6 slices black pudding

1. Heat the oil in a pan and sauté the onion and celery for about 5 minutes or until the onion is transparent.
2. Add the minced beef, salt, pepper and Worcestershire sauce and cook until the meat is well browned.
3. Preheat the oven to 180°C (350°F/Gas 4).
4. Roll out the pastry and, using two-thirds of it, line a shallow round pie dish.
5. Spoon in the meat mixture and arrange the black pudding slices on top.
6. Roll out the remaining pastry and cover the pie with it, crimping the edges together.
7. Bake for 30-35 minutes or until the pastry is golden.

The Bell Inn, Long Hanborough, Oxfordshire
The countryside around the village of Long Hanborough just before harvest is a pretty sight. Dark green hedges and rows of trees divide the golden fields and the village is peaceful in the warm sunshine of late summer.

The Bell Inn is well-known in the neighbourhood for good simple English country cooking, refreshing ales and a convivial atmosphere.

Right: From the kitchen at the Bell Inn, clockwise from bottom left: Love Apple Cocktail, Huntsman's Game Pies, Guinea Fowl with Tudor sauce (see p. 52), Venison, Beefsteak and Mushroom Casserole (see p. 58), Brandy Pralines (see p. 86), vegetables for Guinea Pie.

Farmer's Rabbit Pie

*From the **Cavendish Hotel**, Baslow, Bakewell, Derbyshire.*

Serves 4

1 large fresh rabbit
2½ cups (20 fl oz) dry red wine
4 bay leaves
185 g (6 oz) onions, chopped
salt and freshly ground pepper
seasoned flour
60 g (2 oz) butter
2½ cups (20 fl oz) brown sauce
  (p. 139)

250 g (8 oz) mushrooms, sliced
200 g (6½ oz) minced pork-veal mixture
2 tablespoons brandy
ground mace
375 g (12 oz) puff pastry
egg wash (1 egg yolk mixed
  with a little cold water)

1. Cut the rabbit into 8 pieces and marinate for 48 hours in a mixture of wine, bay leaves, onions, salt and pepper.
2. Dry the meat, dust it with seasoned flour and fry in the butter to brown.
3. Reduce the marinade by half and add it to the meat.
4. Add the brown sauce and mushrooms, cover and cook for 1½ hours.
5. Preheat oven to 190°C (375°F/Gas 5).
6. Cool the mixture and take the meat off the bones.
7. Make 12 meat balls by combining the minced pork and veal, brandy, mace, salt and pepper and rolling them in your hands.
8. Place the rabbit meat, sauce and meatballs in a pie dish, cover with the rolled out pastry and brush it with the egg wash.
9. Bake in the oven for 30 to 45 minutes or until the pastry is golden brown.

Cornish Pasties

*From **The Coachmakers Arms** in Callington, Cornwall.*

Makes 2 large pasties

Pastry
2 cups (8 oz) flour
pinch of salt
90 g (3 oz) dripping or lard
cold water

Filling
250 g (8 oz) stewing steak,
  chopped into small dice
2 large potatoes, peeled and diced
1 large onion, finely chopped
1 medium turnip, peeled and diced
salt
pepper

1. To make the pastry, sift the flour and salt into a bowl, rub in the dripping with your fingers and add enough cold water to make a stiff dough.
2. Preheat the oven to 220°C (425°F/Gas 7).
3. Mix the chopped vegetables together and sprinkle with salt and pepper.
4. Roll the pastry out into 2 large circles.
5. Place half the vegetables on one half of each circle and put the meat on top.
6. Dampen the edges of the pastry and fold them over, pressing the edges together well.
7. Put the pasties on a baking sheet and bake for 20 minutes, then reduce the oven temperature to 180°C (350°F/Gas 4) and bake for a further hour.

Pastai Ty Mawr

Ty Mawr Pie

*This is a speciality of the **Ty Mawr Restaurant** in Brechfa, Wales. It is an individual pie of rump steak, braised in red wine with onions, mushrooms and herbs.*

Serves 6

1.5 kg (3 lb) rump steak, cubed
2 tablespoons seasoned flour
2 tablespoons vegetable oil
500 g (1 lb) onions, chopped
½ bottle red wine
250 g (8 oz) mushrooms, sliced
salt and pepper
pinch of dried oregano
1 bay leaf
1 bouquet garni

Pastry
500 g (1 lb) flour
pinch of salt
250 g (8 oz) lard
125 g (4 oz) butter
juice of half a lemon
iced water
1 egg, beaten and mixed with a
 little water

1. Preheat the oven to 160°C (325°F/Gas 3).
2. Roll the cubed steak in seasoned flour.
3. Heat the oil and gently fry the onions in it until they are golden brown. Remove them from the pan with a slotted spoon.
4. Increase the heat under the pan and fry the steak until it is browned on all sides. Remove the meat.
5. Pour out all but a thin film of oil and add the wine to the pan, stirring with a wooden spoon until the wine has reduced slightly.
6. Put the meat, onions, mushrooms, wine, seasoning and herbs in a casserole dish and braise in the oven for 45 minutes.
7. Remove the casserole from the oven and allow it to cool. Increase the oven temperature to 200°C (400°F/Gas 6).
8. To make the pastry, sift the flour and salt into a bowl. Add the chopped lard and butter and rub these into the flour with your fingertips.
9. Add the lemon juice and enough iced water to make a firm dough. Allow the dough to rest for 30 minutes in the refrigerator before using.
10. Fill 6 individual pie dishes with the meat mixture (first removing the bouquet garni and bay leaf).
11. Roll out the pastry fairly thickly and cover each pie with the pastry. Make decorative leaves with pastry offcuts and place these on top of the pie.
12. Make a slit in the centre of each pie for the steam to escape and brush the pastry with the egg and water mixture.
13. Bake in the oven for 30 minutes. Serve in the pie dishes.

Melton Mowbray Pork Pie

Serves 8

1 kg (2 lb) pork shoulder meat,
  diced into ½ cm (¼ inch) pieces
1 teaspoon salt and
  freshly ground pepper
½ teaspoon ground sage
  or 2-3 fresh leaves, chopped
a pinch each of dry mustard and
  allspice
pork and veal bones

2 onions, chopped
1 bay leaf
2-3 sprigs of marjoram and thyme
250 g (8 oz) lard
500 g (1 lb) flour
⅔ cup (5 fl oz) milk mixed half
  and half with water
1 egg, lightly beaten

1. Mix the meat, salt, pepper, herbs and spices and set aside.
2. To make the stock, boil bones, onions, bay leaf, herbs, salt and pepper in 4 cups
    (1 litre) of water for two hours or until the liquid is reduced to 2⅓ cups (18 fl oz).
    Cool, degrease and refrigerate until it starts to jell.
3. To make the pastry, rub 60 g (2 oz) of the lard into the flour mixed with a teaspoon
    of salt until it is the consistency of breadcrumbs.
4. Boil the rest of the fat with the milk and water.
5. Make a well in the mound of flour and while stirring with a wooden spoon, mix in
    the boiling liquid.
6. Knead and leave to rest for 10 minutes.
7. To make the casing or "coffyn", roll out three-quarters of the dough into a circle
    2 cm (¾ inch) thick. Flour the outside of a cake tin and stand it in the centre of the
    dough. Work the dough up the sides of the tin and then gently remove the tin,
    leaving you with a pie casing.
8. Fill it immediately with the meat mixture as it is likely to collapse.
9. Roll out the remaining dough into a circle slightly larger than the diameter of the
    casing, to form the lid.
10. Preheat the oven to 200°C (400°F/Gas 6).
11. Dampen the top edge of the pie and gently press on the lid. Crimp the edge. Make
    a hole in the centre of the lid and decorate it with pastry leaves.
12. Place on a baking dish and bake in the preheated oven for 20 minutes and then
    reduce the heat to 150°C (300°F/Gas 2) and bake for 1¾ hours. If necessary place
    some aluminium foil on the top to prevent burning.
13. Remove from the oven and allow to cool completely. Pour the chilled stock
    through the hole in the lid and refrigerate.
    Serve cold.

*Right: The Chef, Charles Somerville, at the Black Bull proudly displays his fine dishes,
clockwise from bottom left: Freshwater Crayfish Soup, Roast Beef and Yorkshire
Puddings (see p. 56), Brandy Snaps (see p. 88), Swaledale cheeses, Turbot in pastry.*

The Black Bull Inn, Moulton, Yorkshire

The landlord at the Black Bull Inn is a very impressive gentleman. Towering in height, he carries the weight of a man who really enjoys his food.

My first impression when I arrived, was not very favourable. He had no intention of spoiling what was to be a dinner party for his guests because of a cookbook writer who had travelled some ten thousand miles to photograph his roast beef. The excellence of the beef came first and all other considerations came second. Finally all worked out for the best, I got my shots and the guests, including myself, were served the best roast beef and Yorkshire pudding I had ever eaten.

Mr Kerr turned out to be a very generous host who, in anticipation of my visit, had invited some friends to eat the food that was prepared for photography. He assembled us at a long table in a charming glass-roofed room of his restaurant and treated us to a freshwater crayfish soup. The roast was served with crisp steamed vegetables and was followed by some exquisite local cheese which was presented in 3 stages of aging. Throughout the meal we tasted a line-up of first class German and French wines.

Beef Steak and Kidney Pie

*From **The Anglers' Rest**, Fingle Bridge, Exeter.*
What distinguishes the Devonshire Beef Steak and Kidney Pie from other regional pies is the clotted or double cream which is poured through the hole in the lid just before serving.

Serves 4-6

Pastry
4 cups (1 lb) flour
pinch of salt
125 g (4 oz) margarine
125 g (4 oz) lard
cold water
egg wash (1 egg yolk mixed with a little cold water)

Filling
500 g (1 lb) stewing steak
125 g (4 oz) kidneys
2 onions, chopped
beef stock (see p. 138)
salt
pepper
2 tablespoons cream

1. To make the pastry, sift the flour and salt together into a bowl.
2. Cut the margarine and lard into small pieces and rub it into the flour with your fingertips.
3. Add enough cold water to make a firm dough. Refrigerate until ready to use.
4. Cut the steak and kidney into small cubes, discarding all fat.
5. Put the meat, onion, salt and pepper into a pan and cover it with beef stock.
6. Bring to the boil and then simmer for about 2 hours or until the meat is tender.
7. Preheat the oven to 180°C (350°F/Gas 4).
8. Roll out the pastry into two rounds and line a 20 cm (8 inch) pie dish with one of them. Spoon the steak and kidney into it and cover with the remaining pastry, pressing the edges down well. Cut a hole in the centre of the top crust.
9. Paint the pie with egg wash and bake for 1 hour or until the pastry is golden brown.
10. Just before serving, pour the cream through the hole in the crust.

Note: It's a good idea when preheating the oven to heat up a baking tray at the same time. The bottom crust of the pie, cooked on the hot tray will cook quickly and be much less likely to become soggy.

Our Game Pie

*This is a speciality of **Invereshie House**, Kincraig, Inverness-shire, Scotland.*

Serves 6-8

1 kg (2 lb) stewing venison, diced
125 g (4 oz) bacon, finely chopped
2 onions, chopped
2 carrots, chopped
4 pigeons or 6 quail
1-2 cups (8-16 fl oz) dry red wine
3 sprigs parsley, chopped

2-3 sprigs of several fresh herbs, chopped
1 clove garlic, crushed
salt and freshly ground pepper
puff pastry
egg wash (1 egg yolk mixed with a little cold water)

1. Preheat oven to 180°C (350°F/Gas 4).
2. Place all ingredients except puff pastry and egg wash in a casserole, cover and cook in the preheated oven for about 1½ hours.
3. When cool take the meat off the bones and chop it.
4. Increase the temperature of the oven to 220°C (425°F/Gas 7).
5. Place all the ingredients in a pie dish, cover with the rolled out puff pastry, decorate the top with pastry leaves and roses, brush it with egg wash and bake in the oven until golden brown.

Stargazy Pie

*From **The Coachmakers Arms** in Callington, Cornwall.*
It is said that the best pilchards have always come off the Cornish fishing boats and for
centuries the pilchard industry has flourished. In the Stargazy pie whole fish are used and
while the head is inedible it does contain oils which add to the flavour of the dish.

Serves 4

8-10 small fresh pilchards,
   herrings or mackerel
salt
pepper
3 tablespoons finely chopped parsley
1 cup (4 oz) dry breadcrumbs

3 slices bacon, rinds removed
6 eggs
½ cup (4 fl oz) cream
125 g (4 oz) short crust pastry (see
   p. 141)
egg wash (1 egg yolk mixed
   with a little cold water)

1. Scale the fish, leaving their heads on. Open them out flat, remove their backbones and season the inside with salt and pepper.
2. Put a generous amount of parsley into each cavity and press the fish into shape again.
3. Butter a pie dish and sprinkle with a thick layer of breadcrumbs. Put half the fish on top of this then another layer of breadcrumbs.
4. Arrange the remaining fish so that their heads face the centre of the pie dish and cover with the bacon.
5. Beat the eggs well and mix them with the cream.
6. Pour this over the fish.
7. Preheat the oven to 220°C (425°F/Gas 7).
8. Roll out the pastry and cover the pie with it. Make slits in the pastry and pull out the heads of the fish so that they are looking upwards.
9. Brush the pie with egg wash and bake for 15 minutes then reduce the oven temperature to 180°C (350°F/Gas 4) and cook for a further 45 minutes. Serve hot.

Squab Pie

In Cornwall and Devon in the 18th century, squab took on the meaning of mutton or lamb and
squab pie is made in these counties in this way, without squab or pigeon. This recipe comes
*from **The Coachmakers Arms** in Callington, Cornwall.*

Serves 4-6

500 g (1 lb) stewing lamb or mutton,
   cut into cubes
500 g (1 lb) apples, peeled,
   cored and sliced
¾ cup (4 oz) currants or sultanas
500 g (1 lb) onions, finely chopped
1 tablespoon brown sugar

salt
pepper
water
125 g (4 oz) short crust pastry
   (see p. 141)
egg wash (1 egg yolk, mixed with a
   little cold water)

1. Preheat oven to 220°C (425°F/Gas 7).
2. Put layers of the lamb, apples, currants and onions into a pie dish, sprinkle with the sugar, salt and pepper and pour in just enough cold water to moisten it.
3. Roll out the dough and cover the pie dish with it. Brush with egg wash.
4. Bake for 15 minutes then lower the oven temperature to 180°C (350°F/Gas 4) and bake for a further 1¾ hours.
5. Serve hot.

DESSERTS

Puddings have always been popular in Britain. So much so that today *pudding* is the collective word for any dessert.

Sweet suet puddings are not as popular as they were in the past, but they're still a delicious and comforting winter dessert and it would be hard to imagine a British Christmas without its Christmas Pudding. Other well-known suet puddings are the roly-poly type such as Spotted Dick, Black Treacle Roll and Wet Nelly.

Many tarts, pies and pastries originated in Britain. Open or covered, large or small, they form part of county cooking and their names give away their origins: Cumberland Rum Nicky, Yorkshire Treacle Tart, Banbury Apple Pie, Bakewell Tart, Edinburgh Tart and many others. Custards and trifles are of mediaeval origin and today are as popular as ever. I like the Scottish version of trifle where fruit syrup and Drambuie are mixed in equal parts. Cornish Burnt Cream is a rich custard using cream and clotted cream.

Syllabubs and fools are typically British and are a light and pleasant way of finishing a meal. In the simple syllabub, sugar, lemon juice, sherry and brandy are combined, heated whipped cream is added and the mixture is served in tall glasses. The cream and wine separate and it is drunk through the creamy froth like Irish coffee.

Jellies have always been popular desserts. In Victorian times they were formed into magnificent and elaborate shapes. Fruit and berry juices were frequently used, while port or claret jelly was a popular and elegant dessert.

Edensor Pancakes

*From the **Cavendish Hotel**, Baslow, Bakewell, Derbyshire.*

Serves 4

Batter
¼ cup (1 oz) ground almonds
¾ cup (3 oz) flour
2 eggs, beaten
⅔ cup (5 fl oz) milk
60 g (2 oz) butter, melted

Filling
3 fresh peaches, skinned, stoned and sliced
1¼ cups (10 fl oz) cream, whipped
1½ tablespoons brandy
1½ tablespoons Benedictine
125 g (4 oz) grated dark chocolate
½ cup (4 fl oz) cream

1. Preheat oven to 200°C (400°F/Gas 6).
2. To make the batter combine the almonds, flour, eggs and milk.
3. Stir in the butter.
4. Make 12 pancakes and set aside.
5. To make the filling, combine the peaches, cream, brandy and Benedictine.
6. Divide between the 12 pancakes and fold them into 4.
7. Place the pancakes in a decorative ovenproof dish and put them in the oven for a few minutes until the cream starts to melt.
8. Make a chocolate sauce by melting the chocolate and combining it with the cream.
9. Serve with the sauce.

Right: Guinness Christmas Pudding (see p. 136), Peil Wyke Raspberry Syllabub (see p. 85).

Strawberry Muffins

From the **Hunters' Lodge Restaurant**, *Broadway, Worcestershire.*

Serves 4-6

½ cup (4 oz) caster (powdered) sugar
500 g (1 lb) strawberries, sliced
1¼ cups (10 fl oz) cream, stiffly
  whipped
Muffins
500 g (1 lb) flour
pinch of salt

2 teaspoons sugar
1¼ cups (10 fl oz) warm milk
2 teaspoons dry yeast
1 egg, well beaten
30 g (1 oz) butter, melted
icing (confectioners) sugar for garnish

1. Sprinkle sugar over strawberries and refrigerate for 30 minutes.
2. Fold in cream and return to refrigerator until ready to use.
3. To make the muffins combine the flour and salt.
4. Dissolve the sugar in the milk and add the yeast. Stand in a warm place for 10 minutes.
5. Add the yeast mixture and the egg to the flour, stir in the melted butter and knead for 10 minutes to a soft dough.
6. Place the dough in an oiled bowl, cover and leave to rest in a warm place until it has doubled in size.
7. Turn out onto a floured board, punch it down and roll it out 1.5 cm (½ inch) thick.
8. Cut it into 7.5 cm (3 inch) rounds, place them on a floured board, dust them with flour, cover with a teatowel and leave until double in size.
9. Lightly grease a hot griddle and cook the muffins for about 8 minutes on each side.
10. To serve, split the muffins in half, toast on both sides, spread one side with butter, heap the strawberries and cream on the bottom half, place the other half on top and sprinkle with icing sugar.

Cranachan

This recipe comes from **The Open Arms Hotel** *in Lothian, Scotland.*

Cranachan is very Scottish, served traditionally at Halloween when charms with special significance were folded into the mixture. You might find a ring for marriage, a button for bachelorhood, a thimble for spinsterhood, coins for wealth and horseshoes for luck. Unfortunately my Cranachan at the Open Arms contained none of these, but the flavour combination of lightly toasted oatmeal, cream, sugar and whisky was very Scottish!

Serves 6-8

1¼ cups (4-6 oz) pinhead oatmeal
5 cups cream, beaten until thick
honey

whisky
strawberries or any fresh fruit in
  season
petticoat tails or shortbread biscuits

1. Preheat the oven to 180°C (350°F/Gas 4).
2. Put the oatmeal in a baking dish and bake until lightly brown.
3. Mix the oatmeal and cream together, flavour with honey and whisky according to your taste.
4. Serve in individual glass dishes topped with strawberries and garnished with a petticoat tail.

Hufen Rhosyn
Rose Cream

*From **Ty Mawr** in Brechfa, Wales.*

Serves 4-6

4 egg yolks
1½ tablespoons caster (powdered) sugar
1¾ cups (15 fl oz) milk, scalded
500 g (1 lb) raspberries

1 tablespoon rosewater
15 g (½ oz) gelatine, dissolved in 2 tablespoons cold water
whipped cream for decoration

1. Cream the egg yolks and sugar together until they are thick and pale coloured.
2. Pour the milk over them and put the mixture into a saucepan. Heat it, stirring constantly, until it thickens. Do not allow it to boil.
3. Cool it over a bed of ice.
4. Stir in the gelatine.
5. Reserve a few of the raspberries for decoration and put the rest in a blender or food processor and purée. Pour it through a sieve into the custard mixture.
6. Add the rosewater and mix well.
7. Pour the mixture into a lightly oiled jelly mould and leave it to set in the refrigerator.
8. When it has set, unmould it and decorate it with reserved raspberries and whipped cream.

Pwdin Mynwy
Monmouth Pudding

*From the **King's Head Hotel** in Monmouth, Wales.*

Serves 4-6

6 cups (12 oz) fresh white breadcrumbs
3 tablespoons sugar
4 drops vanilla essence

⅔ cup (5 fl oz) boiling milk
2 tablespoons melted butter
3 egg whites, stiffly beaten
500 g (1 lb) strawberry or raspberry jam

1. Place the breadcrumbs into a warmed bowl and pour the boiling milk over them. Cover the bowl and leave it to stand for 15 minutes.
2. Preheat the oven to 120°C (250°F/Gas ½).
3. Stir the breadcrumb and milk mixture with a fork and add the sugar and melted butter.
4. Fold the beaten egg whites gently into the mixture.
5. Grease an ovenproof dish with butter and spread half the jam on the bottom of it.
6. Spoon half the breadcrumb mixture on top of the jam, then spread over the remaining jam and finally the remaining breadcrumb mixture.
7. Bake for 30 minutes and serve either hot or warm.

Grandmother's Birthday Pudding

*From **The Coachmakers Arms** in Callington, Cornwall.*

Serves 4-6

4 cups (1 lb) flour
pinch of salt
pinch of grated nutmeg
185 g (6 oz) suet, grated
3 cups (1 lb) mixed fruit
milk

Filling
¾ cup (4 oz) brown sugar
1 cup (8 fl oz) whipped cream

1. Mix all the dry ingredients in a large bowl.
2. Add the milk, a little at a time until you have a stiff dough.
3. Spoon the dough into a greased pudding basin, cover the top with foil, tie it down with string and steam in a pan half full of boiling water for 2 hours.
4. Turn the pudding out onto a serving dish and scoop out a little of the centre.
5. Fill the hole with brown sugar and whipped cream and serve piping hot.

Baked Devonshire Apple Dumplings

*From **The Anglers' Rest**, Fingle Bridge, Exeter.*
The name dumpling is a misnomer, as in this Devon speciality, pastry is wrapped around the apple and then it is baked, while normally one would expect to boil dumplings.

Serves 4

250 g (8 oz) sweet short crust pastry
(see p. 141)
4 apples, each weighing about 125 g
(4 oz)
¼ cup (2 oz) sugar

4 cloves
1 egg yolk, mixed with a little cold
water

1. Preheat the oven to 180°C (350°F/Gas 4).
2. Roll out the pastry fairly thinly and cut it into 4 squares big enough to completely enclose an apple.
3. Peel and core the apples, fill their centres with sugar and pierce each one with a clove.
4. Place an apple on each pastry square, brush the edges of the pastry with water and fold it over to completely seal the apple.
5. Decorate the tops with offcuts of pastry cut into shapes.
6. Brush the pastry with the egg yolk and water mixture.
7. Place the apples on a lightly greased baking sheet and bake for 30 minutes or until the pastry is golden brown.
8. Serve with whipped cream.

Right: Clockwise from bottom left: Trout with bacon, Tournados Glantraeth (see p. 58), Anglesey Mushrooms (see p. 28), St. Tudno's Pork (see p. 65), Supreme of Chicken Llandrillo, Potes Cig (see p. 13).

The Chequers Hotel, Northophall Village, Mold, Clwyd

The Chequers is a 19th century Welsh manor house converted into a comfortable country hotel. It is situated in a historical countryside. North Welsh food is served here.

*Potes Cig means Meat Broth and in the past it was customary to serve the meat, potatoes and vegetables for the mid-day meal. The broth was kept for breakfast on the following day when it was served with pieces of bread or broken up oatcake when it was called **brwes**. Indeed simple peasant or workman's fare.*

However, Brithyll yr Afon gyda Chig Moch which despite the long name is just Trout with Bacon is a more interesting dish having an unusual combination of spinach and raisins.

Bakewell Pudding

*From the **Cavendish Hotel**, Baslow, Bakewell, Derbyshire.*
The Cavendish Hotel is only a few miles from Bakewell where this famous dish originated.

Serves 8

250 g (8 oz) sweet short pastry
  (see p. 141)
30 g (1 oz) raspberry jam
4 eggs

½ cup (4 oz) sugar
125 g (4 oz) butter, melted
1¼ cups (4 oz) ground almonds

1. Preheat oven to 200°C (400°F/Gas 6).
2. This dish is usually made in a traditional oval Bakewell pudding tin with sloping sides, however, a 20 cm (8 inch) flan may be used instead.
3. Line the greased dish or flan with the pastry.
4. Cover the pastry with the jam.
5. Beat the eggs and sugar until the mixture is pale and creamy.
6. While stirring constantly, pour the butter into it.
7. Mix in the almonds and pour it over the jam.
8. Bake in the preheated oven for 30 to 35 minutes or until the filling has set.

Devonshire Junket

*From **The Anglers' Rest**, Fingle Bridge, Exeter.*

Serves 6-8

1 litre (4 cups) milk
¾ cup (5 fl oz) brandy
60 g (2 oz) sugar
2 tablespoons rennet

1 cup (8 fl oz) Devonshire clotted cream
  (thickened cream)
¼ tablespoon cinnamon
2 tablespoons sugar

1. Warm the milk and brandy to blood temperature.
2. Stir in the sugar and rennet.
3. Leave to set.
4. Just before serving, garnish with the clotted cream and sprinkle with cinnamon and sugar. The junket may also be decorated with apricot or strawberry jam.

Cotswold Syllabub

*From **The Bell Inn**, Long Hanborough, Oxfordshire.*

Serves 6

2½ cups (20 fl oz) cream
125 g (4 oz) caster (powdered) sugar
juice of 2 lemons

grated rind of 1 lemon
4 tablespoons dry white wine

1. Whip the cream with the sugar.
2. Mix in the lemon juice, rind and wine.
3. Put into tall glasses and chill for 2 to 3 hours before serving.

Cherry Pie

*From the **Bush Hotel**, Farnham, Surrey.*

Serves 6

Pastry
2 cups (8 oz) flour
¼ cup (2 oz) sugar
pinch salt
185 g (6 oz) butter or margarine
1 egg, beaten
1 egg yolk, beaten

Filling
1 kg (2 lb) ripe cherries, stoned
125 g (4 oz) sugar
water
1 tablespoon arrowroot
1 tablespoon Cherry Heering

1. To make the pastry, put the flour, sugar and salt in a bowl and rub in the butter with your fingertips until the mixture resembles coarse breadcrumbs.
2. Add the egg and form into a ball.
3. Refrigerate until ready to use.
4. Place the cherries and sugar in a saucepan and add enough cold water to almost cover them.
5. Bring to the boil and simmer until the sugar has dissolved and the cherries are cooked.
6. Mix the arrowroot with a little of the cooking liquid and add it to the pan.
7. Cook for a further 2-3 minutes, until the sauce has thickened slightly.
8. Set the mixture aside to cool.
9. Preheat the oven to 200°C (400°F/Gas 6).
10. Roll the pastry into 2 rounds. Line a 20 cm (8 inch) pie dish with one round and spoon in the filling.
11. Cover the pie with the remaining pastry, brushing the edges with water and pressing down firmly.
12. Decorate the top of the pie with pastry leaves and brush with beaten egg yolk.
13. Bake for 30-40 minutes or until the pastry is golden brown.
14. Remove the pie from the oven, make a slit in the middle of the pastry and pour in the Cherry Heering.
15. Serve hot with whipped cream.

Peil Wyke Raspberry Syllabub

Syllabubs are a traditional English dessert in which wine, sherry or brandy is mixed with whipped cream. They are usually made several hours before they are served to permit the liquid to separate from the cream.
*This recipe comes from the **Pheasant Inn** in Cumberland.*

Serves 6-8

2½ cups (20 fl oz) cream
½ cup (4 oz) caster (powdered) sugar
315 g (10 oz) fresh raspberries

4 egg whites
150 ml (5 fl oz) dry white wine

1. Whip the cream until it is thick, then fold in the caster sugar.
2. Put the raspberries in a pan with a tablespoon of water and stew over gentle heat for a few minutes. Leave to cool.
3. Whip the egg whites until they form stiff peaks and fold them into the cream mixture.
4. Gently fold the raspberries and wine into the cream mixture and spoon the mixture into champagne glasses. Serve decorated with a raspberry and a raspberry leaf.

Apple and Bramble Fool

*The combination of a fruit purée and cream was once considered foolish, hence the name. Different types of fruit are used and the dessert is very popular in many parts of England. This recipe comes from the **George Hotel** in Chollerford, Northumberland.*

Serves 4-6

250 g (8 oz) Granny Smith apples,
  peeled, cored and sliced
155 g (5 oz) blackberries
¼ cup (2 fl oz) water

½ cup (4 oz) sugar
2½ tablespoons cornflour (cornstarch)
1 cup (8 fl oz) milk

1. Put the apples and blackberries in a pan with the water and ⅓ cup of the sugar. Bring slowly to the boil, stirring until the sugar has dissolved, then simmer until the mixture has reduced to a purée.
2. Mix the cornflour with a little of the milk to make a smooth paste.
3. Put the remaining milk and sugar into a pan, heat and stir until the sugar has dissolved then bring to the boil.
4. Add the cornflour mixture and boil for 3 minutes.
5. Cool the milk mixture slightly and add the fruit.
6. Pour into tall glasses and refrigerate until set. Serve decorated with whipped cream and cherries.

Brandy Praline

*From **The Bell Inn**, Long Hanborough, Oxfordshire.*

Serves 6

500 g (1 lb) Digestive biscuits, crumbed
125 g (4 oz) butter
125 g (4 oz) cooking chocolate

½ cup (4 oz) sugar
2 eggs
¼ cup (2 fl oz) brandy

1. Place the biscuits in a mixing bowl.
2. Over slow heat, melt the butter, chocolate and sugar.
3. Beat the eggs and brandy together.
4. Add the chocolate and egg-brandy mixtures to the biscuits.
5. Beat until they form a thick mixture.
6. Press it into a shallow tray, work it into a square and freeze it.

Chester Pudding

*From the **Waterside Restaurant** in Romiley, Manchester.*

Serves 6-8

1 cup (4 oz) self-raising flour
125 g (4 oz) shredded suet
2 cups (4 oz) soft breadcrumbs
¼ cup (2 oz) caster (powdered) sugar

⅓ cup (4 oz) blackcurrant jam
1 egg, lightly beaten
milk

1. Mix all the dry ingredients together with the jam.
2. Add the egg and enough milk to make a smooth dough.
3. Spoon the mixture into a greased 5 cup (1.25 litre) pudding basin and steam over hot water for 3 hours. Serve with blackcurrant jam.

Right: The fields at the back of the Bell Inn, Long Hanborough, Oxfordshire.

Minted Apple Fool

From the **Hunters' Lodge Restaurant**, *Broadway, Worcestershire.*

Serves 4

**2 large cooking apples,
  peeled and cut into pieces**
½ cup (4 fl oz) water
½ cup (4 oz) caster (powdered) sugar

juice of ½ lemon
16 fresh mint leaves
¾ cup (6 fl oz) cream, stiffly whipped

1. In a saucepan combine the apples, water, sugar, lemon juice and half the mint leaves.
2. Cover and simmer for approximately 15 minutes or until the apples are soft.
3. Purée and rub through a fine wire sieve.
4. Cool, refrigerate for 2 to 3 hours, fold in the cream and serve in glass bowls decorated with the remaining mint leaves.

Brandy Snaps

Traditional English biscuits, they appear in many parts of the country under different names. They are called Mothering Sunday Wafers in Hampshire, in parts of the West Country they are known as Honiton or West Country Fairings, while in Yorkshire they appear as Ormskirk Gingerbread. This recipe comes from **The Black Bull Inn**, *in Moulton, Richmond, Yorkshire.*

Makes 12-16

250 g (8 oz) butter
1¼ cups (8 oz) caster (powdered) sugar
**250 g (8 oz) golden syrup (light corn
  syrup)**
1½ cups (6 oz) flour

½ teaspoon powdered ginger
1 tablespoon brandy
whipped sweetened cream

1. Preheat the oven to 180°C (350°F/Gas 4).
2. Boil the butter, sugar and syrup together until the liquid starts to froth and rise in the pan.
3. Take off the heat and beat in the flour, ginger and brandy until the mixture is smooth.
4. Drop teaspoons of mixture 15 cm (6 inches) apart on greased baking sheets and bake until golden brown in the preheated oven for about 10 minutes.
5. Allow to cool and roll the still soft biscuit around a cream horn mould or greased handle of a wooden spoon.
6. When cold and crisp remove and store in an airtight jar or tin. Just before serving fill the centres with cream.

Cumberland Rum Nicky

This is what is known as a plate pie, i.e. a two-crust pie with a fruit filling. It appears in many parts of England with various fillings.
*This recipe comes from the **Parkend Restaurant** in Wigton, Cumbria.*

Serves 6-8

375 g (12 oz) short crust pastry
  (see p. 141)
1⅔ cups (8 oz) stoned dates, chopped
1½ cups (8 oz) sultanas or seedless
  raisins
60 g (2 oz) butter

⅓ cup (2 oz) soft brown sugar
30 g (1 oz) stem ginger, finely chopped
2 cooking apples, peeled and diced
3 tablespoons rum

1. Preheat the oven to 190°C (375°F/Gas 5).
2. Roll out the pastry thinly, and, using two-thirds of it, line a 23 cm (9 inch) flan ring.
3. Mix all the remaining ingredients together, spoon them into the pastry shell, smoothing the mixture out well.
4. Cover the pie with the remaining pastry, seal the edges, prick the top with a fork, brush with milk and sprinkle brown sugar lightly over the top.
5. Bake for 20 minutes or until the pastry is crisp and golden.
6. Serve warm or cold with lightly whipped cream.

Cumberland Rum Butter

*From **Yan Tyan Tethera** in Keswick, Cumbria.*
The tale goes that a ship from the Cumbrian coast had collected its cargo of spices, rum and sugar from the West Indies, called on Ireland for butter, and then came across a storm which loosened the various barrels and the resultant mixture tasted so good it became a Cumbrian speciality.
Traditionally rum butter is served at christenings or, with whipped cream added, with Christmas pudding.

Serves 6

500 g (1 lb) dark brown sugar
220 g (7 oz) butter, softened
1 teaspoon mixed spices

1 teaspoon cinnamon
¼ cup (2 fl oz) Jamaican rum

1. Cream the sugar and butter together until it is light.
2. Add the spices, cinnamon and rum.
3. Form into a block, wrap in foil and keep in the refrigerator.

CAKES AND BREAD

The rise and development of the very English institution, the afternoon tea party, gave a great boost to the popularity of cakes.

Early English cakes were spiced sweet breads and they were baked for special, mostly religious, feasts such as Easter, Christmas, birthdays, christenings, weddings etc.

In time, more ingredients were added to the bread dough, including finer types of flour, until finally, cakes contained honey or later sugar, dried fruit and spices. Buns, scones, pikelets and crumpets, are types of early cakes.

Yeast was commonly in use until the 19th century but the introduction of chemicals such as bicarbonate of soda soon displaced yeast from cake batters and nowadays little yeast is used. The sponge cake was developed in the 19th century before artificial rising agents were introduced. Its capacity to rise relies on the aeration caused by beating the eggs and sugar.

Biscuits were originally flat, hard pieces of bread which were baked twice. Now a wide range exists, from plain water biscuits through a colourful variety of cookies, oatcakes and the famous Scottish shortcakes.

Gingerbreads are of ancient origin and in the early days were made from crumbled or grated bread, combined with ginger, aniseed, liquorice, honey, ale or wine and dried until hard. Later types were baked and in the 19th century, bicarbonate of soda was introduced.

Devonshire Apple Cake

*From **The Anglers' Rest**, Fingle Bridge, Exeter.*
Devon is well known for its apples and they are used in many local dishes. However, nowhere do they taste as well as in the Devonshire Apple Cake, especially as it was baked and served at the Anglers' Rest.

Serves 6

2 cups (8 oz) self-raising flour	**⅓ cup (2 oz) currants**
¾ cup (4 oz) brown sugar	**250 g (8 oz) peeled and chopped apple**
125 g (4 oz) butter	**milk**

1. Preheat the oven to 220°C (425°F/Gas 7).
2. Put the flour and sugar into a bowl and rub the butter into it with your fingertips.
3. Add the currants and apple, and if the mixture is too dry, add a little milk.
4. Grease a 20 cm (8 inch) cake tin and press the mixture well into it.
5. Bake for 10 minutes at 220°C (425°F/Gas 7) then reduce the temperature to 140°C (275°F/Gas 1) and cook for a further hour.
6. Sprinkle with a little extra brown sugar before serving.

Right: The Anglers' Rest, Fingle Bridge. Clockwise from bottom left: Devonshire Apple Cake (see p. 90), Cider Baked Pork Chops (see p. 68), Devonshire Clotted Cream, Junket (see p. 84), Scones, Beef Steak and Kidney Pie (see p. 76), Baked Devonshire Apple Dumplings (see p. 82).

Carmarthen Yeast Cake

*From **Ty Mawr** in Brechfa, Wales.*

Serves 6

250 g (8 oz) flour
1 teaspoon mixed spice
pinch of salt
1½ cups (8 oz) mixed dried fruit
45 g (1½ oz) butter
45 g (1½ oz) lard
⅓ cup (3 oz) caster (powdered) sugar

2 teaspoons golden syrup (light corn syrup)
1 egg
⅔ cup (5 fl oz) milk, warmed
15 g (½ oz) fresh yeast
½ teaspoon bicarbonate of soda (baking soda)

1. Sift the flour, mixed spice and salt into a large bowl. Add the dried fruit.
2. In another bowl, beat the butter, lard, sugar and syrup together until it is creamy. Add the egg and mix well.
3. Dissolve the yeast in half the warmed milk and the bicarbonate of soda in the other half.
4. Add both mixtures to the creamed butter mixture and beat thoroughly.
5. Fold this butter-yeast mixture into the flour and mix to a soft dough.
6. Preheat the oven to 220°C (425°F/Gas 7).
7. Put the dough into a greased loaf tin and leave in a warm place until it has doubled in size.
8. Bake it for 1½-2 hours or until a skewer inserted in the centre comes out clean.
9. Cool on a wire rack and serve in slices, spread with butter.

Chorley Cakes

*From the **Waterside Restaurant**, Romiley, Manchester.*

Makes 4 cakes

500 g (1 lb) rich short crust pastry (see p. 141)

¾ cup (4 oz) currants
icing (confectioners') sugar

1. Preheat the oven to 180°C (350°F/Gas 4).
2. Roll the pastry out 6 mm (¼ inch) thick and cut into 4 rounds the size of a dinner plate.
3. Place the currants in the centre of the circles, moisten the edges of the pastry with water and bring the edges together in the centre, pressing to seal well.
4. Roll out the cakes until the currants show through, keeping to the round shape.
5. Place the rounds on baking trays and bake for 30 minutes.
6. When cool, sprinkle with icing sugar.

Westmorland Dream Cake

*From **Yan Tyan Tethera** in Keswick, Cumbria.*

Serves 6

Base
1 cup (4 oz) flour
125 g (4 oz) butter
2 tablespoons soft brown sugar

Topping
1½ cups (8 oz) soft brown sugar
¼ cup (1 oz) plain (all-purpose) flour
pinch salt
1 cup (4 oz) walnuts, chopped
1 cup (3 oz) desiccated coconut
½ teaspoon baking powder
2 eggs, beaten

1. Preheat the oven to 180°C (350°F/Gas 4).
2. Rub the butter into the flour and then add the sugar, mixing in well.
3. Press this mixture into a Swiss (jelly) roll tin and bake for 20 minutes. Allow to cool.
4. To make the topping, mix together all the dry ingredients then mix in the eggs.
5. Spread the mixture on top of the cooled base and bake a further 20 minutes or until it browns.
6. Leave to cool in the tray before cutting into slices.

Saffron Cake

*From the **Coachmakers Arms**, Callington, Cornwall.*

Serves 6-8

4½ cups (1 lb 2 oz) flour
pinch of salt
125 g (4 oz) butter
125 g (4 oz) lard
⅓ cup (3 oz) sugar
pinch of freshly grated nutmeg

pinch of saffron
1⅔ cups (8 oz) currants
⅓ cup (2 oz) mixed peel
15 g (½ oz) fresh yeast
warm milk

1. Sift the flour and salt into a bowl and rub the butter and lard into it with your fingertips.
2. Add the sugar, nutmeg, saffron, currants and peel and mix well.
3. Put the yeast into a cup with a pinch of sugar and a little warm milk.
4. When the yeast mixture becomes foamy, make a well in the centre of the flour mixture and pour the yeast into it.
5. Beat the mixture well, adding enough warm milk to make a soft dough.
6. Leave the mixture to rise in a warm place until it has doubled in bulk.
7. Preheat the oven to 180°C (350°F/Gas 4).
8. Put the mixture into a greased loaf tin and bake for 50-60 minutes or until it is cooked through.
9. Cool on a wire rack and serve sliced with butter.

Yorkshire Parkin

*From **The Black Bull Inn**, Moulton, Richmond, Yorkshire.*

Serves 6

½ cup (3 oz) brown sugar
90 g (3 oz) margarine
185 g (6 oz) golden syrup
  (light corn syrup)
185 g (6 oz) medium oatmeal
1½ cups (6 oz) flour

½ teaspoon mixed spices
½ teaspoon ginger
½ teaspoon bicarbonate of soda
  (baking soda)
1 egg

1. Preheat the oven to 180°C (350°F/Gas 4).
2. Melt the sugar, margarine and syrup together.
3. Add the dry ingredients, mix well and beat in the egg.
4. Pour the mixture into a shallow cake tin and bake in the preheated oven for approximately one hour. When cold cut into squares. (The Chef recommends that it be kept for at least 2 days in an airtight tin before serving).

Tipsy Hedgehog

*From the **Waterside Restaurant**, Romiley, Manchester.*

Serves 6

500 g (1 lb) Digestive (wheatmeal)
  biscuits
125 g (4 oz) dark (semi-sweet)
  chocolate, grated

2½ cups (20 fl oz) port wine
whipped cream

1. Line a bowl with foil and press in the biscuits and half the grated chocolate.
2. Pour in the port and allow it to soak in the refrigerator overnight.
3. Turn out onto a serving dish, shape into a 'hedgehog' shape and coat in whipped cream. Decorate with the remaining grated chocolate.

King's Head Hotel, Monmouth

It is not certain which King's head is meant, but in any case be it Henry V who was born in Monmouth Castle or Charles I who was a frequent visitor there, the King's Head Hotel boasts a long and distinguished history.

Today it is an elegant and comfortable place, which occasionally serves regional Welsh dishes.

Leeks are said to be the Welsh national vegetable so it is not surprising that wherever one goes it appears in one form or other. At the King's Head it was offered in Carol Cennin a Hufen which I am told was Creamed Leek Soup served with sippets and diced meat. Blue Shell Cockles were deep fried in a batter and served with a Tartare type sauce.

Leeks re-appeared in Wyau Aron (Anglesey Eggs) where they were mixed in with mashed potatoes.

Trout Agincourt, obviously honouring Henry V the victor of Agincourt who was also known as 'Harry of Monmouth', is a delicious stuffed fish combining prawns from the nearby sea and the trout from local rivers.

IRELAND

INTRODUCTION

In search of a lost tradition.

Historically, nobody would suggest that the Irish have had a sheltered existence, so it is interesting to note that while the people of Ireland have been knocked about in one way or another, their eating habits have remained almost unchanged for hundreds of years.

The Romans, who exerted a strong influence wherever they went, did not quite make it across the Irish sea, the Normans had their hands full in England so that they, too, left no mark on local eating habits. Ireland also missed out on the returning Crusaders bringing back the many interesting and tasty spices and unknown oriental delicacies which are absorbed into the European cooking repertoire.

The Irish climate is temperate and the soil fertile, so that for centuries, while nobody but the landlords lived in luxury, nobody, thanks to good crops and plenty of dairy herds, pigs and sheep, had to starve.

The sixteenth century saw the introduction of the potato by Sir Walter Raleigh. Easy to cultivate, growing underground and reasonably protected from adverse external conditions, it soon became the mainstay of Irish cooking with the major part of the cuisine containing potatoes in one form or another.

Irish cooking was in the true sense of the word, a peasant cuisine where products grown by the individual were the basis of their own cooking. The ingredients were simple: potatoes, vegetables from the garden around the house, buttermilk and curds from their own cow, their own honey which was the main sweetening agent, apples and berries from the surrounding trees and bushes. Those along the shores supplemented their diet with the catch from the sea. Recipes were handed down by word of mouth and there were only slight regional variations.

Today, very few traditional dishes are offered in public eating places. There is the occasional and delicious Irish Stew, and Boxty Bread and Pancakes make an appearance, but there is nothing on the scale of many Continental countries where regional food is the pride of the table.

What has happened to traditional Irish Cooking? During my recent visit there, I asked that question many times and I think that there is an answer.

During the last two hundred years, traditional Irish cooking, the simple but wholesome fare of the Irish farmhouse, has been associated with poverty and misfortune. When people started to become more prosperous, they discarded Irish food in favour of new, foreign flavours. The result is that today a great effort will have to be made to search out what little can be found of the old and forgotten traditions. The older generation may still hold the memories of the food of their childhood, but unless a concerted effort is made soon, a valuable cultural asset will be lost forever.

Nowadays, while the wealth of traditional recipes may not be great, modern Ireland has an abundance of first quality products which supply the many ingredients from which good food is created.

Some of the best seafood can be found in the coastal waters around Ireland. The Dublin Bay Prawn, not a prawn at all but a small type of Norwegian lobster, bred all year round, is probably the most famous and certainly the most delicious local product of the sea.

Cockles, scallops and oysters, especially those from County Galway, have a quality of their own, while sole and mackerel deserve the reputation they enjoy.

Local hams are good and that from Limerick, smoked with juniper branches and berries, has a taste of its own.

Famous also are the Irish salmon and local trout. Lamb and pork are tasty too and being mainly an agricultural country, so are most other products including the inevitable potato.

Tony Annammy

SOUPS

Irish soups are as old as the hearth. In the past as well as today they are an important and substantial part of Irish meals. Being of farmhouse origin, they are simple yet filling, and at times of famine they contained whatever little was available. Often they consisted only of water, bacon and potatoes. Bacon, when available, was the only meat that large parts of the impoverished country population ever saw. When times were really bad the bacon was taken out of the broth and was served as a separate meal.

In the coastal parts of the country, mussels, cockles and clams were frequently used. When the season was good and vegetables were plentiful, most of these soups were rich, nourishing vegetable broths flavoured with different types of seafood. Some of them, to make them even more filling, were cooked with potatoes. Irish Potato Soup has many regional variations. All are tasty, filling and typical of a country that depended on the potato for its daily food.

Many Irish Soups are a result of extreme austerity such as little soup or grunt soup in which the young of the perch are used. Pigs trotters are called Crubins or Crubeens in Ireland and make a tasty soup. Crubins Pea Soup (see p. 100) is a typical winter soup, combining pig's trotters and dried peas.

Irish Potato Soup

Serves 6

1 kg (2 lb) potatoes, peeled and diced	**salt**
2 large onions, sliced	**freshly ground pepper**
90 g (3 oz) butter	**1¼ cups (10 fl oz) milk**
5 cups (1.25 litres) water	**2 tablespoons cream**
3 tablespoons mixture of finely chopped parsley, thyme and sage	**2 tablespoons chopped chives or mint**

1. Sauté the potatoes and onions in the butter for approximately 15 minutes but do not brown.
2. Place them in a large saucepan, add water, herbs, salt and pepper and simmer for approximately 30 minutes until the vegetables are tender. Remove from the heat and allow to cool.
3. In a blender or food processor purée the mixture.
4. Transfer to the saucepan, add the milk and bring to the boil.
5. Serve hot garnished with cream and the chopped chives or mint.

Gregan's Castle Hotel, Ballyvaugham, Co. Clare

I had been told about the Burren but it wasn't until I was actually driving right through the middle of it that I realised the uniqueness of this barren limestone plateau.

Historically and botanically the area is unique. Its appearance has hardly changed since prehistoric times. The portal dolmens, stone ring forts of later years, early Christian foundations and Norman Castles bear witness to 4500 years of human habitation. The fissures and crevices of the almost waterless bare terrain shelter unusual and rare fauna.

Gregan's Castle is situated at the edge of this fascinating and unique area and overlooks Galway Bay.

Here, under Peter and Moira Harden's supervision, some fine local food is served.

Right: Irish Stew (see p. 122) and Irish Soda Bread (see p. 130) are displayed in front of a cosy logfire at Gregan's Castle.

Mussel Soup

Serves 6

4 dozen mussels
60 g (2 oz) butter
2 tablespoons flour
4 cups (1 litre) of the water from the mussels
2 cups (16 fl oz) milk

2 tablespoons chopped parsley
2 stalks celery, chopped
salt
freshly ground pepper
½ cup (4 fl oz) cream

1. Clean the mussel shells thoroughly and place them in a large saucepan. Cover and simmer for approximately 5 minutes until the shells open. Do not continue cooking once the shells are open.
2. When the mussels have cooled remove them from their shells and reserve them.
3. In a saucepan melt the butter, add the flour and gradually add the cooking water from the mussels and the milk, stir constantly making sure the mixture is smooth. If there is not enough water from the mussels add milk or water.
4. Add the parsley, celery, pepper and salt and cook for 10 to 15 minutes.
5. Just before serving add the mussels, heat gently and serve with the fresh cream.

Crubins Pea Soup

Also called Crubeens, the Irish name for pig's trotters.

Serves 6

3 pig's trotters
500 g (1 lb) dried peas, soaked overnight
8 cups (2 litres) water
1 bunch celery, chopped

3 onions, chopped
1 bay leaf
6 peppercorns
salt
chopped fresh herbs or parsley for garnish

1. Simmer the pig's trotters for 3 hours.
2. Add the rest of the ingredients and simmer for a further hour.
3. Take out the trotters, cool them, pick off all the meat, chop it roughly and set it aside.
4. Rub the vegetables and liquid through a fine sieve.
5. Return the meat to the soup, reheat, adjust seasoning if necessary and serve it hot, sprinkled with herbs or parsley.

Bacon and Cabbage Pea Soup

Serves 6

250 g (8 oz) bacon, diced
125 g (4 oz) dried peas, soaked
  overnight
5 cups (1.25 litres) cold water
½ cabbage shredded
1 large carrot, sliced

½ turnip, sliced
1 large onion, sliced
salt
freshly ground pepper
6 slices toast

1. Place the bacon and the soaked peas in a large saucepan and add the water.
2. Simmer for 1½ hours and skim off the scum and fat.
3. Add the cabbage, carrot, turnip and onions and simmer for a further 45 minutes, season.
4. Place one slice of toast in each of the soup plates, pour the soup over and serve immediately.

Leek and Potato Soup

Serves 6

2 leeks, white part only, sliced
60 g (2 oz) butter
1 kg (2 lb) potatoes, peeled and
  sliced
salt
freshly ground pepper

6 cups (1.5 litres) half milk
  and half chicken stock (see p. 138)
1 cup (4 fl oz) cream
2 tablespoons chopped chives or
  parsley
6 rashers bacon, chopped and fried
  until crisp

1. In a saucepan sauté the leeks in butter but do not brown.
2. Add the potatoes and season. Add the milk and stock mixture, cover and simmer for one hour. Cool the soup.
3. Purée the soup in a blender or food processor.
4. Add the cream, reheat but do not boil.
5. Serve hot garnished with the chopped chives or parsley and the fried bacon.

Irish Turnip Soup

Serves 6

3 large turnips, chopped
1 large onion, chopped
60 g (2 oz) butter
4 cups (1 litre) chicken stock
  (see p. 138)
2 cloves

¼ cup (1 oz) flour
2 cups (16 fl oz) milk
2 teaspoons sugar
salt
freshly ground pepper

1. Place the turnips, onions and butter in a heavy-bottomed saucepan. Cover and cook gently for 30 minutes.
2. Add the chicken stock and cloves, cover and simmer for a further 30 minutes. Discard the cloves.
3. Purée the mixture in a blender or food processor and return to the saucepan.
4. Mix the flour to a smooth paste with some of the milk.
5. Add the flour, the milk and sugar and season. Cook for a further 10 minutes.

FIRST COURSES

In traditional Irish cooking, there are no clear divisions into courses as there are in French or Italian cuisines.

In recent times, it has become acceptable to serve, in addition to or instead of soups, certain light, appetizing and savoury dishes. Frequently these consist of seafood which, in Ireland, is of first class quality.

The famous Galway oysters are eaten fresh with some freshly ground pepper and a few drops of lemon juice, or they are made into a delicious soufflé.

Kippers, smoked trout and the noble Irish smoked salmon are served to excite the appetite at the beginning of the meal. Dublin Bay prawns are amongst the best-known of Irelands' seafood and they too form part of many first course dishes.

In Ireland, traditionally every part of a beast is eaten and therefore it is not surprising to find a number of dishes prepared with offal, many of which have been adopted for the start of the meal.

Galway Oyster Soufflé

Serves 4

24 oysters
juice of ½ lemon
½ cup (2 oz) fresh breadcrumbs
½ cup (4 fl oz) cream

2 egg yolks, lightly beaten
salt and pepper
pinch of mace
2 egg whites, stiffly beaten

1. Oysters in shells or bottled oysters may be used. Chop 20 of the oysters and save 4 for garnish.
2. Mix the oyster liquid and lemon juice, heat it and pour it over the breadcrumbs, stir in the chopped oysters, cream and egg yolks. Season and add mace.
3. Fold in the egg whites.
4. Pour the mixture into one large or several individual buttered soufflé dishes. Do not fill them right to the top. Cover with aluminium foil, place them in a baking dish filled with hot water, cover the dish with foil and steam them over medium heat for 1 hour for the large basin and 40 to 45 minutes if using small dishes. To serve, turn them out onto plates and serve hot.

The Basil Bush, Ballydehob, Co. Cork
At the Basil Bush, Shirley Foster and Alfie Lyons bake their sour-dough bread daily and from whatever fresh ingredients happen to be available, they put together their own style of cooking.

Fresh fish from the nearby sea or trout from local rivers, good local meat and fresh vegetables find their way to the Basil Bush Kitchen.

Right: Poached trout, salads and home baked sourdough bread.

Sweetbreads and Bacon

Serves 6

6 sweetbreads
salt
3 slices bacon, cut in two
1 onion, finely chopped

3 tomatoes, peeled and sliced
1 cup (8 fl oz) chicken stock
  (see p. 138)
4 sprigs parsley, chopped

1. Preheat oven to 180°C (350°F/Gas 4).
2. Soak the sweetbreads in water for 30 minutes.
3. Salt the water, bring it to the boil and simmer the sweetbreads for 8 minutes.
   Strain and cool them and remove the membrane.
4. Wrap a piece of bacon around each sweetbread and secure it with a toothpick.
5. Place them in a buttered ovenproof dish on a bed of onion and tomato slices.
6. Add the stock, sprinkle with half of the parsley and pepper and bake in the
   preheated oven for 35 to 45 minutes.
7. Serve hot sprinkled with fresh parsley.

Irish Rarebit

Serves 4

2 cups (8 oz) grated (Irish) Cheddar
  cheese
15 g (½ oz) butter
⅓ cup (2 fl oz) milk
½ tablespoon vinegar

1 teaspoon mustard
salt and freshly ground pepper
30 g (1 oz) chopped gherkins
slices of buttered toast

1. In a saucepan combine cheese, butter and milk. Heat and stir until it is creamy.
2. Add vinegar, mustard, salt, pepper and gherkins.
3. Spoon the mixture on the toast and brown it under a preheated grill, serve hot.

Kippers on Toast

Serves 4

250 g (8 oz) kipper fillets, flaked
2 tablespoons cream
2 hard-boiled eggs, chopped
salt and freshly ground pepper

juice of ½ lemon
2 sprigs parsley, finely chopped
4 slices of buttered toast

1. Combine kippers, cream, eggs, salt, pepper, lemon juice and parsley.
2. Spoon it on to the pieces of toast and heat it under a hot grill. Serve it garnished with lemon twists and olives.

Closheens (Scallops) in White Wine

Serves 4

15 g (½ oz) butter
1 onion, finely chopped
1 clove garlic, crushed
1 tablespoon flour

1¼ cups (10 fl oz) dry white wine
4 sprigs parsley, finely chopped
2 sprigs thyme, finely chopped
salt and freshly ground pepper
24 scallops

1. In a saucepan melt the butter, add the onion and garlic and sauté until it is soft and transparent.
2. Add the flour and cook it for 2 to 3 minutes without browning it.
3. Gradually stir in the wine and add half the parsley, the thyme, salt and pepper. Cook for 5 minutes.
4. Add the scallops and over low heat cook for a further 3 minutes.
   Serve hot sprinkled with the remaining parsley.

VEGETABLES

While the potato is the best known of Ireland's vegetables, the fertile soil, combined with a moist yet temperate maritime climate, produces a wide variety of vegetables.

In the country, most houses have their own vegetable garden where, with the seasons, fresh vegetables for the kitchen are grown. Vegetables are, in fact, the most important ingredient in Irish cooking.

Colcannon is among the most typical of vegetable dishes. It combines potatoes, cabbage, leeks and sometimes turnips and carrots mashed together with plenty of butter and cream. It has that true Irish flavour.

Bacon is frequently used to add flavour, especially to cabbage which is plentiful and among the most popular of vegetables.

The Irish share their liking for leeks with their Welsh neighbours across the Irish Sea.

While seaweed may not be to everybody's liking, laver salad with a dressing of oil, vinegar, salt and pepper is most unusual.

Most dishes are simple, permitting the true flavour of each vegetable to stand on its own.

Potato Cakes

Makes 8-10 cakes approximately 7.5 cm (3 inches) in diameter.

200 g (7 oz) self-raising flour
45 g (1½ oz) butter
mashed potatoes made from
 300-400 g (10-13 oz) potatoes

¼ cup (2 fl oz) milk
1 tablespoon caraway seeds
salt

1. Preheat the oven to 230°C (450°F/Gas 8).
2. Combine the salt and the flour and mix in the butter with your hands.
3. Add the mashed potatoes and mix them thoroughly with the flour.
4. Gradually pour in the milk to make a soft dough.
5. On a floured board, roll out the dough approximately 2.5 cm (1 inch) thick.
6. With a biscuit cutter approximately 7.5 cm (3 inches) in diameter, cut the dough into cakes. Sprinkle each cake with caraway seeds.
7. Arrange the cakes on a baking dish and bake them in the preheated oven for approximately 20 to 30 minutes.
8. Traditionally the cakes are eaten hot, split through the middle and spread with butter.

Right: Potatoes and leeks, the 'Irish' vegetables.

Potato Pudding

Serves 6

½ cup (2 oz) flour
60 g (2 oz) butter, melted
500 g (1 lb) mashed potatoes

2 eggs
¾-1¼ cups (6-10 fl oz) milk
salt and freshly ground pepper

1. Preheat the oven to 110°C (225°F/Gas ¼).
2. Mix the flour and butter into the mashed potatoes.
3. Stir in the eggs and enough milk to make the mixture sloppy. Season to taste.
4. Spoon it into a buttered ovenproof dish, cover and bake in preheated oven for 6 hours.

Leeks in Cream Sauce

Serves 4

8 leeks, white parts only, split in half
   and washed
50 g (1⅔ oz) butter

½ cup (2 oz) flour
½ cup (4 fl oz) cream
salt
pepper

1. Preheat oven to 200°C (400°F/Gas 6).
2. Boil the leeks in salted water for 10 minutes or until they are tender, save the water.
3. To make the sauce, melt the butter and stir in the flour. Cook for 2 to 3 minutes without browning.
4. Add enough of the hot leek cooking water to make a thick smooth sauce. Simmer for 5 minutes.
5. Add cream and season to taste.
6. Arrange the leeks in an ovenproof dish and pour the sauce over.
7. Bake in the preheated oven until the top turns light brown.

Colcannon

Serves 4

1 kg (2 lb) potatoes,
  peeled, boiled and mashed
250 g (8 oz) mashed cooked cabbage
2 small leeks cooked and mashed
30 g (1 oz) butter

1 tablespoon finely chopped onion
2 tablespoons cream
salt
freshly ground pepper

1. Place the potatoes in a large bowl and, while beating with a wooden spoon, add the cabbage and the leeks. Mix in the butter and onion and finally add the cream. If the mixture is too thick, more cream or milk may be added. Season to taste.
2. Place this mixture in a saucepan and heat gently for approximately 5 minutes.

Champ

Irish Mashed Potatoes

Serves 4

8 potatoes
1 onion, thinly sliced
1½ cups (12 fl oz) milk or buttermilk

4 spring onions, finely chopped
90 g (3 oz) butter
salt and freshly ground pepper

1. Boil the potatoes in salted water until soft. Drain.
2. Cook the onion in the milk for 5 minutes.
3. Pour the milk and onion on to the potatoes and mash them until creamy.
4. Beat the spring onions, butter, salt and pepper into the potatoes. Serve hot.

Pratie Oaten

Potato Oat Cakes

Serves 6

1⅔ cups (8 oz) oatmeal
500 g (1 lb) mashed potatoes
salt and freshly ground pepper

milk
melted butter

1. Combine oatmeal, potatoes, salt, pepper and enough milk to make a firm dough.
2. Sprinkle some oatmeal on a board and roll out the mixture approximately 2 cm (¾ inch) thick.
3. Cut it into small rounds, triangles or squares and cook on a hot griddle or fry them in butter. Serve hot with melted butter.

FISH

No part of Ireland is too far from the coast, so that fresh saltwater fish and seafood are readily available throughout the country.

Inland rivers and lakes abound with trout, perch and in season with the finest of salmon, which has a reputation equal to its Scottish cousin. Eaten fresh, simply fried or grilled, its flesh is firm and sweet. In Dublin I have also eaten some delicious smoked salmon of exceptional quality and flavour.

When the fish is of good quality there is little need for sauces and strong garnishes. Grilled Irish lobster with melted butter is unsurpassed.

Herrings have always been plentiful and are readily available. Fresh or pickled, they appear in many dishes. Mackerel are also popular and are sometimes used instead of herrings.

The Dublin Bay prawn is famous. Its delicate flavour is best appreciated when simply cooked and served with the least embellishment. Not really a prawn at all, but a Norway lobster, it is a relative of the Adriatic scampi.

Equal in well deserved reputation is the lemon sole, eaten fresh, simply grilled or fried with butter, lemon juice and parsley. There is also black sole which is the same as the very tasty Dover sole.

The best oysters in Ireland come from the oyster beds along the coast of Galway. Oysters are best when eaten freshly opened and with pepper, salt and lemon juice. Every year Galway has a famous oyster festival during which the fastest oyster openers gather from all over the world and try their skills.

Prawns with Mushrooms

Serves 4

250 g (8 oz) button mushrooms, sliced	salt
60 g (2 oz) butter	freshly ground pepper
¼ cup (1 oz) flour	500 g (1 lb) uncooked, shelled prawns
1 cup (8 fl oz) cream	1 tablespoon Irish whiskey

1. In a saucepan fry the mushrooms in the butter.
2. Sprinkle the mushrooms with the flour and mix well.
3. Lightly heat the cream and while continuously stirring pour it over the mushrooms and cook until creamy.
4. Add the prawns and continue simmering for 3 to 5 minutes.
5. Before serving, check the seasoning, sprinkle with the Irish whiskey and serve with boiled rice.

Jury's Hotel, Dublin

Jury's Hotel is one of Dublin's best hotels of international standard and its kitchens are under the direction of executive chef Michel Treyvand.

Unfortunately Irish regional dishes do not find their way to the hotel's menu, which is a pity as I am certain that travellers from other countries who are staying there would love to taste some local food.

However, local products such as Dublin Bay prawns, lobsters, fresh and smoked salmon are presented in grand style. As an hors d'oeuvre, smoked salmon cornets filled with cooked Dublin Bay prawns and served with a smooth rich mayonnaise were delicious.

Right: Chef Michel Treyvand with a platter of smoked salmon and Dublin Bay prawns, and above, cold poached fresh salmon in aspic, garnished with lobster.

King Prawns in Whiskey Sauce

*From **Marlfield House** in Gorey, Co. Wexford.*
Marlfield House is a beautifully restored Regency period house which was originally the Dower House on the estate of the Earls of Courtown. Comfortable and elegant it is surrounded by acres of gardens and woodland.
The hostess, Mary Bowe, serves some fine seafood which comes from the nearby coast. Her fresh salmon is particularly good, while home made cakes and ice creams provide a fitting ending to the meal.

Serves 4

30 g (1 oz) butter
30 g (1 oz) onions, chopped
1 small capsicum (pepper), chopped
15 g (½ oz) flour
30 g (1 oz) tomatoes, peeled and
   chopped
1 clove garlic, chopped

1 tablespoon fennel leaves, chopped
salt
freshly ground pepper
⅔ cup (5½ fl oz) dry white wine
250 g (8 oz) fresh king prawns
¼ cup (2 fl oz) Irish whiskey

1. In a frying pan melt the butter and sauté the onions and capsicum until they are soft but not brown.
2. Stir in the flour, add the tomatoes, garlic, fennel and seasoning.
3. Add the wine and the shelled prawns and cook for 3 to 5 minutes.
4. Finally add the whiskey and cook for a further 2 minutes.
5. The prawns and sauce are usually served with boiled rice.

Deep Fried Prawns

Serves 6

1 kg (2 lb) king prawns
   with tails and shells removed and
   deveined
bacon slices cut in 3
2 egg yolks
2-3 cups (16-24 fl oz) beer or stout
1 tablespoon melted butter

salt and pepper
1½ cups (6 oz) flour
2 egg whites, whipped until stiff
flour
oil for deep frying
mayonnaise with finely chopped
   gherkins

1. Wrap each prawn in a piece of bacon and secure it with a toothpick.
2. To make the batter combine the yolks, beer and butter and whip lightly. Add the salt and pepper and mix it into the flour. Mix until it is a smooth coating batter. Fold in the egg whites.
3. Dust the prawns with flour, dip them in the batter and deep fry in hot oil until the batter is crisp and golden brown.
4. Drain on kitchen paper and serve with mayonnaise.

Scallop Mushroom Potato Pie

Serves 4

12 scallops
1 cup (4 fl oz) milk
salt
freshly ground pepper
30 g (1 oz) butter
1 tablespoon flour

250 g (8 oz) mushrooms, sliced
4 tablespoons sweet sherry
cold mashed potatoes
   made from approximately 500 g
   (1 lb) potatoes
1 tablespoon chopped parsley

1. Preheat the oven to 180°C (350°F/Gas 4).
2. Simmer the scallops in the milk with some salt and pepper for 2 to 3 minutes. Strain and reserve the milk.
3. Melt the butter in a saucepan, add the flour and cook for 2 to 3 minutes without browning it. Gradually add the warm milk making sure that the mixture is smooth.
4. Add the mushrooms, sherry and the scallops. Transfer everything into an ovenproof dish and cover the top with the mashed potatoes.
5. Dot the potatoes with some butter and bake in the preheated oven for approximately 20 to 30 minutes or until the top has browned.
6. Serve garnished with the chopped parsley.

Dressed Crab

*This recipe is featured at **Ballymaloe House** in Shangarry, Co. Cork.*
Myrtle Allan, who with her husband Ivan, runs the Hotel and Restaurant, is the author of the
'Ballymaloe Cookbook' which is a collection of recipes from her repertoire at Shangarry. No
wonder then, with such a competent cook presiding over the kitchen, that Ballymaloe House
enjoys such a reputation for good food – regrettably only some of it Irish. Mrs Allan notes in
her book that 500 g (1 lb) cooked crab in a shell will yield about 120-180 g (4-6 oz) of crab
meat.

Serves 4-6

3 cups crab meat
   (2 or 3 crabs should yield this)
1¾ cups (3½ oz) soft breadcrumbs
½ tablespoon white vinegar
2 tablespoons fruit chutney
30 g (1 oz) butter

1 generous pinch dry mustard
salt
freshly ground pepper
½ cup Béchamel sauce (see p. 140)
1 cup (4 oz) fine dry breadcrumbs
60 g (2 oz) butter

1. Preheat the oven to 200°C (400°F/Gas 6).
2. Mix together all ingredients except the dry breadcrumbs and butter, and taste for seasoning.
3. Pack the mixture into the crab shells, top it with the breadcrumbs and cover it with dobs of butter.
4. Place the crab shells in the preheated oven and cook until thoroughly heated through and browned on top — approximately 20 to 30 minutes.

Clarinbridge Oyster Stew

Serves 4

3 dozen oysters	2 cups (16 fl oz) milk
60 g (2 oz) butter	2 cups (4 oz) white breadcrumbs
salt	½ tablespoon paprika
freshly ground pepper	juice of ½ lemon
1 bay leaf	2 tablespoons chopped parsley

1. Open the oysters, clean them and save the juice.
2. In a saucepan lightly sauté the oysters in the butter for not more than 2 to 3 minutes. Season with salt and pepper and add the bay leaf, milk and juice of the oysters.
3. Cook for a further two or three minutes.
4. To thicken, add the breadcrumbs.
5. Finally add the paprika and lemon juice and serve garnished with the chopped parsley.

Fish and Bacon

The original recipe was for ling, a member of the cod family, but any white fish may be used.

Serves 6

1 kg (2 lb) fish, (one large or 3 small fish)	salt and freshly ground pepper
30 g (1 oz) butter	250 g (8 oz) bacon slices
	finely chopped parsley for garnish

1. Preheat the oven to 180°C (350°F/Gas 4).
2. Arrange the cleaned and scaled fish in a buttered ovenproof dish, dot with butter and season.
3. Cover the fish with the bacon. Cover with aluminium foil and bake in the preheated oven for 30 minutes.
4. Increase the heat to 200°C (400°F/Gas 6) and remove the foil. Bake for a further 15 minutes to brown the bacon.
5. To serve place the fish and bacon on a heated serving platter. Pour any coating juices over and garnish with parsley.

Paddy Bourke's, Clarinbridge, Co. Galway

Like most coastal towns of Ireland, Clarinbridge has excellent seafood. It is also the town where the annual Galway Oyster Festival takes place.

Needless to say, Paddy Bourke's (Ireland's most famous Oyster Tavern) specialises in seafood and on the menu the hungry traveller will find – well, oysters and the delicious Clarinbridge Chowder.

Smoked Salmon is served with home-made brown bread baked in true Irish tradition.

Local sole, scallops and shrimp combine in a house speciality called Symphony of the Sea. A Smoked Cod Casserole with vegetables is recommended and of course there is also Paddy Bourke's version of Irish Stew.

The restaurant has a very pleasant atmosphere and is popular among the locals as well as attracting travellers in search of good seafood.

Right: Clockwise from bottom left: Irish Stew, Poached Salmon with Asparagus, Symphony of the Sea, Clarinbridge Oyster Stew (see p. 114), Smoked Cod Casserole, Mushroom Soup, Homemade brown bread.

Baked Galway Cod with Mussels

Serves 4

3 dozen mussels
1 kg (2 lb) cod, cut into steaks
salt
freshly ground pepper
2 tablespoons chopped thyme
12 small potatoes, cooked

8 small onions, cooked
60 g (2 oz) melted butter
1 tablespoon chopped parsley
1 tablespoon chopped fennel
4 slices of lemon

1. Preheat the oven to 200°C (400°F/Gas 6).
2. Clean the mussels and place them in a saucepan with a little water, cover and cook for approximately 5 minutes until the mussels are open. Cool the mussels.
3. Remove the mussels from the shells and set aside. Reserve the liquid.
4. Place the cod steaks in a greased baking dish, season and sprinkle with the thyme.
5. Place the cooked potatoes and onions around the fish. Add the melted butter to the mussel liquid and pour it over the fish.
6. Bake in the preheated oven for approximately 20 minutes.
7. Serve the fish topped with the mussels and sprinkled with the chopped parsley and fennel. Decorate it with the lemon slices.

Baked Trout with Cream and Cucumber

Serves 4

4 plate-sized trout
60 g (2 oz) softened butter
3 sprigs parsley, chopped
salt

freshly ground pepper
1 cup (8 fl oz) cream
1 large cucumber, peeled,
    seeded and cut into small cubes
juice of 1 lemon

1. Preheat the oven to 185°C (350°F/Gas 4).
2. Rub the trout with the softened butter and sprinkle them with parsley, salt and pepper. Pour the cream around the trout, cover the baking dish with a lid or foil and bake it in the preheated oven for 15 minutes.
3. Remove from oven and add the cucumber and lemon juice.
4. Return to oven for a further 15 minutes.
5. To serve, arrange the trout on a serving dish and pour the cream and cucumber over the fish.

Creamed Fish

Serves 4

8 fillets of any white fish
seasoned flour
½ cup (4 oz) melted butter
½ cup (4 fl oz) cream

½ cup (4 fl oz) milk
1 teaspoon made up English
  mustard
chopped parsley for garnish
4 lemon wedges

1. Dust the fish with flour and dip them in the butter.
2. Place them in a shallow pan and pour in the cream and milk, season.
3. Gently bring to the boil, reduce the heat to low and simmer for 10 minutes.
4. Place the fish on a preheated serving platter and keep warm.
5. Simmer the liquid until it reduces and thickens.
6. Mix in the mustard, pour it over the fish, sprinkle with parsley and serve it garnished with lemon wedges.

Jellied Eel

Serves 4-6

1 kg (2 lb) eels
3-4 cups (24-32 fl oz) water
3 bay leaves
juice of 1 lemon
2 onions, chopped

salt and freshly ground pepper
¼ teaspoon nutmeg
pinch of mixed spices
30 g (1 oz) gelatine
3 sprigs dill, chopped

1. Skin the eels and cut into small lengths.
2. Put them in a saucepan and add enough cold water to cover. Slowly bring to the boil and skim off the scum and fat.
3. Add the bay leaves, lemon juice, onions, salt, pepper, nutmeg and spices.
4. Simmer over low heat for 10 to 15 minutes until eels are cooked.
5. Take out the fish, remove the flesh from the bones and cut it into small pieces.
6. Place them into a bowl or a mould and sprinkle with dill and parsley.
7. Strain the cooking liquid and skim off all fat.
8. Dissolve the gelatine in some of the warm liquid and add it to the rest. Season to taste.
9. Pour it over the fish, cool and refrigerate. Serve with a tossed salad.

MEAT AND POULTRY

Today lush green pastures of the Emerald Isle produce a wide range of livestock and there is no shortage of meat for the table. However, this was not always the case. Most traditional farmhouse dishes were devised to make the best of what little was available. So every part of the slaughtered beast was used. To add substance to the dishes, potatoes, cabbage, turnips, carrots and other vegetables which happened to be in season were used.

Wholesome simplicity denotes most Irish meat dishes. Known all over the world, the Irish Stew is a typical example. Originally made with mutton, as it would be wasteful to use lamb, it combines meat with Ireland's most famous product, the potato. Onions provide the flavour and traditionally no other vegetables are added.

Sausages are a means of making the meat go further and in the Dublin Coddle, a traditional Saturday supper dish, sausages, bacon and potatoes are cooked together.

In the past, pig killing was done in autumn and all parts of the animal were used. The most famous of all pork products is undoubtedly Limerick Ham, first pickled and then smoked over oak shavings, straw and juniper berries. Its flavour is without equal.

Nothing was wasted. Even the stomach, filled with mashed potatoes, sage, onions, salt and pepper, is served with gravy and apple sauce as Irish Pig Haggis, while pig's trotters, known as crubeens, could be bought at the local pub and eaten with soda bread and Guinness.

One of the traditional Christmas dishes is Spiced Beef which nowadays, decorated with holly, can be bought in butcher's shops during the festive season.

Guinness Stout adds a definite flavour to meat and is occasionally used in cooking. Braised Beef in Guinness has gained international recognition and is known in France as ''ragoût à l'Irelandaise.''

Not even Ireland has been spared the curse of the battery reared chickens. Fed scientifically on a diet of processed food, they grow up plump and tender but deprived of the flavoursome meat their farmyard cousin in olden days offered. Traditional Irish poultry recipes successfully supplement this deficiency.

Irish Beef Stew

Serves 4-6

45 g (1½ oz) dripping
500 g (1 lb) shin beef
  cut into 2.5 cm (1 inch) cubes
3 carrots, sliced
2 onions, sliced
3 stalks celery, choppped

¼ cup (1 oz) flour
2 cups (16 fl oz) beef stock (see p. 138)
1 tablespoon tomato paste
salt and freshly ground pepper
8-12 small potatoes
4-6 slices of bacon, cut into large pieces

1. Preheat oven to 160°C (325°F/Gas 3).
2. In a casserole melt the fat and brown the meat all round.
3. Take out the meat and in the remaining fat sauté the vegetables until slightly browned.
4. Mix in the flour, gradually add the stock, mix in the tomato paste and season to taste.
5. Return the meat to the casserole, cover and cook in the preheated oven for 45 minutes.
6. Place the potatoes on top, cover again and continue cooking for a further 45 minutes or until potatoes and meat are done.
7. Grill the bacon and serve the stew out of the casserole topped with the bacon.

Right: Traditional Irish Fare: soda bread and Irish Beef Stew (see p. 118).

Braised Beef with Guinness and Prunes

Serves 6

30 g (1 oz) dripping
1 kg (2 lb) shin beef
  cut into large cubes
2 onions, sliced
3 carrots, sliced
2 tablespoons flour

⅔ cup (5 fl oz) Guinness
⅔ cup (5 fl oz) water
3 sprigs parsley, chopped
3 bay leaves
salt and freshly ground pepper
1 cup (6 oz) soaked prunes

1. Preheat oven to 140°C (275°F/Gas 1).
2. In a casserole heat the fat and brown the meat.
3. Add the onions and carrots and brown them lightly.
4. Add the flour, cook for a few minutes, add the Guinness, water, parsley, bay leaves and seasoning.
5. Cover and cook in preheated oven for 1½ hours. Mix in the prunes and cook for a further hour or until the meat is tender.

Corned Meat and Cabbage

Corned silverside or pickled pork may be used.

Serves 6-8

1.5 kg (3 lb) corned meat,
  soaked in water to remove
  excess salt
2 onions, chopped
2 carrots, sliced
3 stalks celery, chopped

2 sprigs thyme, chopped
2 sprigs parsley, chopped
4 bay leaves
6 peppercorns
1 large cabbage cut into 6-8 pieces

1. In a large saucepan combine all the ingredients except the cabbage and cover with water.
2. Slowly bring to the boil, cover and simmer over low heat for 1 hour. If necessary take off any scum which may float to the top.
3. Add the cabbage and under cover simmer for a further 2 hours.
4. When cooked take out the meat, rest it for 10 minutes, slice it and serve on a serving platter surrounded with the cabbage and vegetables.
   If it's not too salty, the stock can be used to make a lentil or pea soup.

Spiced Beef

A traditional Christmas dish.

Serves 8

1.5 kg (3 lb) silverside or brisket	**freshly ground pepper**
1 cup (8 oz) coarse salt	**½ teaspoon ground bay leaves**
⅓ cup (2 oz) brown sugar	**1 tablespoon saltpetre**
½ teaspoon allspice	**60 g (2 oz) black treacle**
½ teaspoon nutmeg	**250 g (8 oz) carrots, sliced**
½ teaspoon ground cloves	**1 onion, finely chopped**
¼ teaspoon dry thyme	

1. Rub the meat with salt and leave it overnight.
2. Combine the sugar, allspice, nutmeg, cloves, thyme, pepper, bay leaves and saltpetre.
3. Rub the salt off the meat and wipe it dry.
4. Rub the meat with the spice mixture, cover it and refrigerate it for 2 days.
5. Heat the treacle and pour it over the meat.
6. Refrigerate for a week and during that time, every day, rub the treacle and spices firmly into the meat.
7. Roll the meat lightly and tie it firmly with some string.
8. Place it in a saucepan with enough water to cover it. Add carrots and onions and simmer over low heat for 3 hours.
9. Cool it in the liquid. Place it between two plates and press it down with heavy weights overnight. Serve cold and sliced.

Braised Beef with Guinness

Serves 4

1 kg (2 lb) boned shin of beef cut into large cubes	**salt**
30 g (1 oz) butter	**freshly ground pepper**
1 large onion, sliced	**1 tablespoon chopped parsley**
2 tablespoons flour	**4 bay leaves**
1 cup (8 fl oz) Guinness	**250 g (8 oz) carrots, sliced**
	1 cup soaked prunes or raisins

1. Preheat the oven to 150°C (300°F/Gas 2).
2. In a heavy bottomed cast iron casserole, brown the meat in the butter, add the onions and cook until light brown.
3. Sprinkle the meat with flour and let the flour brown.
4. Add the Guinness. The liquid should cover the meat, if there's not enough, add water. Season, add the parsley, bay leaves and carrots.
5. Cover and braise in the preheated oven for 2 hours.
6. Check the seasoning, and half an hour before the end of the cooking time, add the prunes or raisins.

Irish Stew

*from **Gregans Castle** in Ballyvaugham, Co. Clare.*

Serves 4-6

1 kg (2 lb) lamb neck chops
salt
freshly ground pepper
6 medium sized onions, chopped

1 kg (2 lb) potatoes, peeled and sliced
2½ cups (20 fl oz) water
2 tablespoons parsley, chopped

1. Preheat the oven to 175°C (350°F/Gas 4).
2. Place the meat in the bottom of a heavy, cast iron casserole and cover it with a layer of chopped onions and a layer of the sliced potatoes. Add a little water and boil on the top of the stove for 15 minutes.
3. Add the rest of the water, cover the casserole and place it in the oven for one hour.
4. Add the remaining onions and potatoes.
5. Cover again and return to the oven for a further hour, or until the vegetables are cooked and the meat is tender.
6. Serve directly from the casserole, garnished with parsley.

Irish Hunter's Pie

Serves 6

60 g (2 oz) butter
1 onion, finely chopped
1 carrot, finely chopped
2 stalks celery, finely chopped

1¾ cups (14 fl oz) beef stock
 (see p. 138)
6 mutton or lamb chops
1.5 kg (3 lb) mashed potatoes
salt and freshly ground pepper

1. Melt half of the butter and lightly sauté the onion, carrot and celery.
2. Add the stock, place the chops on top, cover and over low heat braise the meat for 30 minutes.
3. Preheat the oven to 200°C (400°F/Gas 6).
4. Lift out the chops and rub the vegetables and liquid through a fine sieve. Reserve the purée.
5. Place two-thirds of the potatoes in a buttered pie dish, place the chops on top, season and cover with the rest of the potatoes. Dot the top with the rest of the butter and bake in the preheated oven until brown.
6. Make a hole in the top layer of potatoes and pour in some of the vegetable purée. Serve the rest with the pie.

Right: Kylemore Abbey in Co. Galway.

Dublin Coddle

Serves 6

6 thick bacon slices
6 pork sausages
1 litre (4 cups) boiling water
3 large onions, sliced
750 g (1½ lb) potatoes,
  peeled and sliced

3 tablespoons chopped parsley
salt
freshly ground pepper

1. Preheat the oven to 150°C (300°F/Gas 2).
2. In a saucepan, boil the bacon and sausages in the water for 5 minutes.
3. Drain the water and reserve it.
4. On top of the sausages and bacon place layers of onions and potatoes and the chopped parsley. Season lightly, keeping in mind the saltiness of the bacon. Cover with the liquid.
5. Cover the saucepan with a lid and place it in the preheated oven for approximately 1 hour. The ingredients must be cooked but not be too soft.
6. Traditionally this dish is served with soda bread and Guinness.

Crubeens
Irish Pig's Trotters

Serves 6

12 pig's trotters
3 stalks celery, chopped
3 onions, chopped
3 carrots, sliced
6 peppercorns
3 bay leaves
½ teaspoon dry thyme

3 sprigs parsley, chopped
salt
flour
2 eggs lightly beaten
¼ teaspoon English mustard
breadcrumbs seasoned with salt and
  pepper
dripping

1. In a large saucepan combine trotters, celery, onions, carrots, peppercorns, bay leaves, thyme, parsley and salt. Add enough water to cover.
2. Bring to the boil, reduce heat to low and simmer for 2½ hours or until the meat is tender.
3. Take the trotters out of the liquid and remove the meat from the bones. Strain and keep the liquid for later use as stock.
4. Dust the meat with flour, dip it in a mixture of egg and mustard and coat it in breadcrumbs.
5. Heat the dripping and fry the meat until brown and crisp. Can be served in a piquant sauce made with stock.

Pickled Pork with Cabbage

Serves 6-8

2 kg (4 lb) pickled pork,
  soaked for 3 hours to remove
  excess salt
2 carrots, sliced
2 large onions,
  stuck with four cloves

4 tablespoons chopped thyme and
  parsley, fresh or dried
12 peppercorns
1 cabbage cut into 6-8 portions

1. Combine all ingredients except the cabbage in a large saucepan, cover with water and bring to the boil.
2. Simmer gently for one hour.
3. Add the cabbage, cover and simmer for further 1½ hours.
4. To serve, cut the pork into small portions, and serve surrounded by the cabbage. The cooking liquid may be used to make a very tasty pea soup.

Pickled or Smoked Tongue with Spicy Sauce

Serves 4

1 pickled or smoked tongue,
  soaked in several changes of
  water for 12 hours
1 onion, chopped
1 stalk celery, chopped
2 cloves
2 teaspoons dried herbs
4 peppercorns
2 bay leaves
1 tablespoon gelatine

Sauce
200 g (6½ oz) redcurrant jelly
1 cup (8 fl oz) stock from the tongue
1 cup (8 fl oz) port
grated rind of 1 lemon and ½ orange
juice of 1 lemon and 1 orange
2 tablespoons vinegar
1 teaspoon mustard powder
1 tablespoon horse-radish

1. In a saucepan combine the tongue, onion, celery, cloves, herbs, peppercorns and bay leaves and add enough water to cover.
2. Bring to the boil, reduce the heat to low and simmer for 3 to 4 hours until the tongue is tender. Allow it to cool in the liquid.
3. Skin and trim the tongue, curl it up in a basin and weigh it down to press.
4. Strain 1½ to 2 cups of the cooking liquid and dissolve the gelatine in it.
5. Pour it around the tongue and refrigerate it until it is set.
6. To make the sauce, combine all the sauce ingredients and boil until the liquid reduces and thickens. Cool the sauce.
7. To serve the tongue, cut it into slices and serve it with the sauce.

Country Style Tripe

Serves 6-8

1 kg (2 lb) tripe cut into 5 cm (2 inch)
  pieces
6 onions, sliced
3 slices bacon, roughly chopped
3 cups (24 fl oz) milk
1 cup (8 fl oz) water

salt
freshly ground pepper
3 tablespoons flour
4 sprigs parsley, chopped
½ cup (2 oz) dry breadcrumbs
30 g (1 oz) butter, melted

1. In a casserole combine tripe, onions, bacon, milk, water, salt and pepper. Cover, bring to the boil, reduce heat to low and simmer for 2 hours.
2. Dissolve the flour in a little of the cooking liquid, and mix it into the tripe. Cover and simmer for a further 30 minutes.
3. Add parsley, sprinkle with breadcrumbs, pour the butter evenly over the breadcrumbs and brown it under a preheated grill.

Stuffed Chicken Breasts

Serves 4

1 onion, finely chopped
6 small mushrooms, chopped
30 g (1 oz) butter
250 g (8 oz) mashed potatoes
salt and pepper
1 egg, lightly beaten

4 chicken fillets
4 slices of bacon
½ cup (4 fl oz) water
½ cup (4 fl oz) liqueur Irish whiskey
flour

1. Preheat oven to 180°C (350°F/Gas 4).
2. Sauté the onions and mushrooms in the butter.
3. Add the potatoes, salt, pepper and egg.
4. Place the fillets on a board, cover them with plastic film and gently beat them flat with a meat mallet.
5. Divide the stuffing equally and place in the centre of the fillets. Roll them and wrap them in bacon. Secure with toothpicks.
6. Place them in a casserole, add the water, cover the dish and braise in the preheated oven for 30 to 35 minutes.
7. Take out and place them on a heated serving plate and keep hot.
8. Add half the whiskey to the cooking juices. Season to taste and thicken slightly with flour.
9. Pour the sauce over the rolls. Heat the remaining whiskey, ignite it and pour it over. Serve immediately.

Right: There are no traditional Irish recipes for quail, so they're most often roasted and served with game chips.

Chicken with Cabbage

1.5 kg (3 lb) chicken cut into 8 pieces
seasoned flour
lard or bacon fat
1 onion, chopped

½ head cabbage, chopped
salt and freshly ground pepper
1 cup (8 fl oz) dry white wine
juice of ½ lemon

1. Dust the chicken pieces in flour and brown them in the hot fat.
2. Place them in a casserole.
3. In the same fat sauté the onions until light golden.
4. Add the cabbage and sauté for a few minutes. Season.
5. Add wine and lemon juice and spoon the mixture into the casserole.
6. Cover and cook over low heat for 45 minutes to 1 hour until the chicken is tender.

Roast Chicken with Bread Sauce

Serves 4

1 1.75 kg (3½ lb) chicken
30 g (1 oz) softened butter
Stuffing
breadcrumbs made from
    4 large slices of white bread
½ cup (4 fl oz) milk
2 tablespoons chopped parsley
1 tablespoon chopped thyme
1 clove garlic, crushed
pinch of nutmeg
salt
freshly ground pepper

Bread Sauce
6 cloves
1 large onion
2 cups (16 fl oz) milk
2 bay leaves
pinch of powdered mace
10 peppercorns
1 cup brown breadcrumbs
15 g (½ oz) butter
2-3 tablespoons cream
salt
freshly ground pepper

1. Preheat oven to 180°C (350°F/Gas 4).
2. To make the stuffing, soak the bread in the milk for 10 to 15 minutes then squeeze out all the liquid.
3. Combine all the ingredients for the stuffing.
4. Fill the cavity of the chicken with the stuffing and with a skewer, close up the opening.
5. Place the chicken on the roasting pan. Rub it with softened butter and roast in the preheated oven for 1¼ hours.
6. Remove the chicken from the baking dish and keep hot.
7. Strain off the fat, add 2 cups of the chicken stock to the cooking juices and continue cooking until it reduces and thickens.
8. To prepare the bread sauce, stick the cloves into the onion and place it in a saucepan with the milk, bay leaves, mace and peppercorns.
9. Boil it gently for approximately 15 minutes and leave it aside for a further 30 minutes so that the liquid can absorb the flavours of the ingredients.
10. Strain the milk into another pan and add the breadcrumbs.
11. Return it to the heat and stir it until the breadcrumbs have absorbed the milk. Continue boiling it gently for 2-3 minutes. Season.
12. Before serving add the butter and the cream.
13. The chicken is served with the bread sauce and the gravy in two separate sauce boats.

Braised Spatchcock with Ale

Serves 4

12 small onions
12 button mushrooms
15 g (½ oz) butter
2 spatchcocks approximately 600 g
 (19 oz) each
250 g (8 oz) ham cubed
1 clove garlic, crushed

3 sprigs marjoram, chopped
salt and pepper
2 cups (16 fl oz) ale (beer)
8 triangular deep fried bread slices
chopped parsley for garnish

1. In a casserole sauté the onions and mushrooms in butter.
2. Add the spatchcocks, ham, garlic, marjoram, salt, pepper and ale.
3. Cover and braise over low heat for 45 to 50 minutes or until the spatchcocks are tender.
4. Cut each bird in half lengthwise, place on the croûtons and sprinkle with parsley.

Stuffed Goose with Apple Sauce

What makes this recipe typically Irish is the use of potatoes in the stuffing.

Serves 8

1 3-4 kg (6-8 lb) goose
1 cup (8 fl oz) chicken stock
 in which the goose giblets have been
 cooked
Stuffing
750 g (1½ lb) cooked, diced potatoes
2 onions, chopped
3 slices bacon, chopped
salt
freshly ground pepper

liver of the goose, chopped
2 tablespoons parsley, chopped
1 tablespoon fresh sage, or 2 teaspoons
 dried
Apple Sauce
250 g (8 oz) peeled, cored apples,
 cut into pieces
½ cup (4 fl oz) chicken stock
30 g (1 oz) butter
1 tablespoon sugar
pinch of nutmeg
salt

1. Preheat oven to 200°C (400°F/Gas 6).
2. Mix all the stuffing ingredients together and put them into the main cavity of the bird. Secure the opening with a skewer.
3. Place the bird, breast side down, on a rack in a roasting pan.
4. Place the roasting pan in the preheated oven and roast for 45 minutes.
5. Reduce the oven temperature to 160°C (325°F/Gas 3) and continue roasting for 1 hour.
6. At the end of the hour, turn the bird breast side up, and roast at the same temperature for 30 to 45 minutes, until the breast is golden brown. During this time, baste with the cooking juices and the stock. If necessary, add a further cup of stock.
7. To prepare the apple sauce, cook the apples in the stock until they are tender. Purée the apples in a blender or food processor. Add the butter, sugar and pinch of nutmeg and serve hot with the goose.
8. The goose should be carved and arranged on a serving platter with the stuffing surrounding the pieces of meat.

BREAD, CAKES AND DESSERTS

Who would have thought of using potatoes in bread and cakes? The Irish did — they were not being frivolous about it but did it out of necessity. The mashed potatoes made the precious flour go further in times when it was in short supply.

Today we all enjoy crisp, hot, tasty Boxty bread with lots of butter, potato cakes with caraway seeds and of course Irish potato scones.

Farmhouse style bread in Ireland is tasty and while most of it is baked with yeast, soda bread, made with bicarbonate of soda is the best known Irish bread speciality. It is essential to use buttermilk or sour milk to get the true flavour.

In general, Irish cakes are quite simple, unsophisticated, but always full of flavour. The chocolate sandwich cake is an example of using mashed potatoes in the preparation of cakes.

The Guinness or Porter cake derives its full flavour from the stout which also keeps the cake nice and moist. Irish whiskey is also sometimes used to give typical flavour.

Carrageen, or Irish Moss is a gelatinous seaweed found off the coast of Ireland and it is used in the preparation of jellies and aspics. Full of vitamins and minerals its health-giving qualities are well appreciated.

The Irish also have a wide variety of biscuits of which the shortcakes strongly compete with their Scottish cousins.

Fresh curd or cottage cheese was frequently used in the making of cheese cakes. Today, as in the Almond Cheese cake (see p. 137), the name remains but the cheese is omitted.

Irish Soda Bread

The traditional recipe requires the use of buttermilk or sour milk, however, if fresh milk is used one teaspoon of cream of tartar should be added to the dry ingredients.
*This recipe comes from **Gregans Castle** in Ballyvaugham, Co. Clare.*

Serves 6

6 cups (1½ lb) flour	**¼ tablespoon salt**
¼ tablespoon bicarbonate of soda	**1 cup (8 fl oz) buttermilk or sour milk**

1. Preheat the oven to 200°C (400°F/Gas 6).
2. Mix all the dry ingredients in a basin and make a well in the centre.
3. Stir in the milk vigorously. If necessary add more milk, but the mixture should not be too thin.
4. On a floured board flatten the dough into a circle approximately 4 cm (1½ inches) thick.
5. With a floured knife make a cross in the dough.
6. Place the baking sheet into the preheated oven for approximately 40 minutes.

   Note: Brown Irish Soda Bread may be made as above but using 500 g (1 lb) wholewheat flour and 250 g (8 oz) plain white flour — a little more milk may be required to mix the dough.

Right: An Irish afternoon tea: scones (see p. 133) and Guinness Cake (see p. 134).

Boxty Bread

Makes 4 cakes

500 g (1 lb) raw potatoes, grated	**salt**
500 g (1 lb) cooked mashed potatoes	**freshly ground pepper**
500 g (1 lb) flour	**¼ cup (2 fl oz) melted bacon fat**

1. Preheat the oven to 160°C (325°F/Gas 3).
2. Place the grated potatoes in a cloth over a basin and wring out as much liquid as possible. Let it stand until the starch has sunk to the bottom.
3. In a bowl, mix the grated potatoes with the mashed potatoes, add the flour, pepper and salt.
4. When the starch has sunk to the bottom, pour off the liquid from the top and scrape the starch into the other ingredients.
5. Add the melted bacon fat and combine all the ingredients thoroughly.
6. Divide the dough into four parts and on a floured board form them into round flat cakes.
7. Make a cross in the top of the cakes and place them on a greased baking dish.
8. Bake them in the preheated oven for approximately 40 to 50 minutes.
9. Serve hot split into four and covered with butter.

Irish Treacle Loaf

⅓ cup (2½ fl oz) water	
60 g (2 oz) butter	**½ teaspoon mixed spice**
60 g (2 oz) black treacle	**½ teaspoon ground ginger**
⅓ cup (2 oz) brown sugar	**1 teaspoon bicarbonate of soda**
1 egg	**⅓ cup (2 oz) currants**
2 cups (8 oz) flour	**⅓ cup (2 oz) raisins**

1. Preheat oven to 180°C (350°F/Gas 4).
2. Heat the water and melt the butter in it.
3. Mix the treacle with the sugar and egg until creamy.
4. Mix the flour, spice, ginger and bicarbonate of soda and add it to the treacle mixture.
5. Stir in the currants, raisins and the water/butter mixture.
6. Pour the dough into a 1 kg (2 lb) bread tin and bake in the preheated oven for 1½ to 2 hours.

Scones

Makes 15 scones

4 cups (1 lb) self-raising flour
pinch of salt
125 g (4 oz) margarine

⅓ cup (3 oz) sugar
milk
1 egg yolk mixed with a little cold water

1. Preheat the oven to 190°C (375°F/Gas 5).
2. Sift the flour and salt into a bowl.
3. Rub in the margarine with your fingertips.
4. Add the sugar and then the milk, a little at a time, until it is a soft consistency.
5. Roll out on a floured board to about 2 cm (¾ inch) thick.
6. Cut into rounds about 6 cm (2½ inches) in diameter and place on a lightly greased baking sheet.
7. Paint with the egg yolk and water mixture and bake for 20 minutes or until they are golden brown.
8. Remove from the oven and cool on a wire rack.

Potato Scones

15 g (½ oz) butter, melted
½ teaspoon salt
250 g (8 oz) cold mashed potatoes

½ cup (2 oz) oatmeal
½ teaspoon baking powder

1. Add the butter and salt to the potatoes.
2. Add enough oatmeal and the baking powder to make a pliable dough.
3. Roll it out thick and using a saucer approximately 14 cm (7½ inches) in diameter, cut it into rounds, prick the top with a fork and score it into quarters without cutting them right through.
4. Cook them on a hot griddle for 3 to 4 minutes each side. Serve hot with butter.

Date and Walnut Crunch

Serves 6-8

1 (250 g/8 oz) packet plain sweet biscuits
125 g (4 oz) margarine
⅓ cup (3 oz) sugar
125 g (4 oz) dates, finely chopped

125 g (4 oz) walnuts, finely chopped
125 g (4 oz) glacé cherries, quartered
200 g (6½ oz) dark chocolate

1. Crush the biscuits in a food processor or with a rolling pin.
2. Melt the margarine in a pan and add the sugar and dates. Stir until the sugar has dissolved.
3. Remove the pan from the heat and add the crushed biscuits, walnuts and cherries.
4. Press the mixture firmly into a greased Swiss (jelly) roll tin and refrigerate until set.
5. Melt the chocolate in a bowl standing in a pan of hot water and spread it over the date and walnut crunch.
6. When the chocolate has set, cut the crunch into squares or fingers and serve.

Guinness Cake

Makes one 20 cm (8 inch) cake

125 g (4 oz) butter
1½ cups (8 oz) brown sugar
3 eggs, lightly beaten
3 cups (12 oz) self-raising flour
pinch of salt
pinch of mixed spice

125 g (4 oz) raisins, soaked
60 g (2 oz) mixed peel,
  chopped and soaked
250 g (8 oz) sultanas, soaked
60 g (2 oz) glacé cherries
½ cup (4 fl oz) Guinness

1. Preheat the oven to 180°C (350°F/Gas 4).
2. Cream the butter and sugar until the sugar is dissolved. Beat in the eggs, add the flour, salt, mixed spice and the soaked dried fruit. Finally mix in the Guinness.
3. Pour the mixture into a greased cake tin.
4. Place the cake tin into the preheated oven and bake for 2 hours. To prevent burning, cover the top with foil for the last ½ to ¾ hour of the baking.
5. When baked, allow it to cool, remove from cake tin and cut into portions.

Chocolate Whiskey Cake

*From **Marlfield House** in Gorey, Co. Wexford*

Serves 6

250 g (8 oz) Digestive biscuits
  (Graham Crackers, Granita)
250 g (8 oz) dark cooking chocolate
250 g (8 oz) butter
2 eggs

⅓ cup (3 oz) caster (powdered) sugar
60 g (2 oz) glacé cherries
60 g (2 oz) walnuts, chopped
½ cup (4 fl oz) Irish whiskey
¼ cup (2 fl oz) whipped cream

1. Crush the biscuits coarsely and set them aside.
2. In a double boiler, melt the chocolate together with the butter.
3. Cream the eggs and sugar until they are light in colour.
4. Add the chocolate and butter to the eggs while stirring constantly.
5. Add ¾ of the glacé cherries and the walnuts, save the rest for garnish. Add all except for one tablespoon of the whiskey and the crushed biscuits.
6. Butter a 23 cm (9 inch) baking dish and pour the whole mixture into the mould.
7. Decorate the top with the remaining cherries and walnuts and place in the refrigerator for several hours. Remove it approximately 30 minutes before serving.
8. Decorate the top of the cake with the whipped cream to which the remaining tablespoon of whiskey has been added.

Jockey Hall, Curragh, Co. Kildare

This very attractive restaurant not far from the famous race course, is run by a very competent chef, Paul McCluskey, who serves very fine Nouvelle Cuisine dishes. Irish Stew is also on the menu and it is a pity that it is the only representative of local cooking. I can imagine that, with Paul McCluskey's dedicated approach to food, Irish national dishes would receive a new lease of life.

Right: Clockwise from bottom left: Roast stuffed breast of veal, rack of lamb, chocolate box cake, fresh salmon terrine with green peppercorns, sole with chives.

Irish Boiled Cake

90 g (3 oz) golden syrup
  (light corn syrup)
⅔ cup (5 fl oz) water
½ cup (4 oz) caster (powdered) sugar
¾ cup (4 oz) currants
¾ cup (4 oz) sultanas
125 g (4 oz) butter

2 cups (8 oz) plain (all-purpose) flour
¾ teaspoon baking powder
1 teaspoon mixed spice
1 teaspoon ground ginger
1 egg, lightly beaten

1. Preheat the oven to 180°C (350°F/Gas 4).
2. In a saucepan combine the syrup, water, sugar, currants, sultanas and butter and boil for 8 to 10 minutes, stirring occasionally. Set aside and cool.
3. Mix together the flour, baking powder, spice and ginger and stir it into the liquid. Mix in the egg.
4. Pour the dough into a baking tin and bake for 1½ to 2 hours or until cooked. Cool the cake on a rack and serve it sliced.

Guinness Christmas Pudding

375 g (12 oz) sultanas
125 g (4 oz) glacé cherries
250 g (8 oz) raisins
125 g (4 oz) mixed peel
1½ cups (8 oz) brown sugar
250 g (8 oz) chopped suet

1 cup (4 oz) flour
2 cups (4 oz) soft breadcrumbs
pinch of salt
pinch of cinnamon
pinch of mixed spice
¾ cup (6 fl oz) Guinness

1. Soak the sultanas, cherries, raisins and mixed peel in water until they are soft.
2. In a mixing bowl, combine the sugar, suet, flour, breadcrumbs, salt, cinnamon and mixed spice and mix until it is the consistency of breadcrumbs.
3. Add the soaked fruit and stir in the beaten eggs. Finally add the Guinness.
4. Mix well and pour the mixture into one large, or two small, greased pudding bowls.
5. Cover with foil and tie down with some string.
6. Steam the pudding for 4 to 5 hours.
7. When completed, remove from the water. Serve immediately or store and re-heat for 1-2 hours before serving.
8. Traditionally, this Irish Christmas pudding is served with Irish Whiskey Butter.

Irish Whiskey Butter

½ cup (4 oz) caster (powdered) sugar
60 g (2 oz) butter

2 tablespoons Irish whiskey

1. Cream the sugar and the butter until the sugar is dissolved, gradually add the whisky. Refrigerate and serve with the pudding which has been flamed with Irish whiskey.

Irish Mist Cream

2½ cups (20 fl oz) milk
4 egg yolks
2 tablespoons honey
7 teaspoons gelatine

¼ cup (2 fl oz) Irish Mist liqueur
1¼ cups (10 fl oz) cream, whipped
4 egg whites, stiffly beaten

1. Bring the milk to boiling point.
2. In a bowl stir yolks and honey together and while continuing to stir, incorporate the milk into the yolk mixture.
3. Pour back into the saucepan and over low heat, stirring it constantly, cook it until the mixture thickens, do not boil.
4. Dissolve the gelatine in warm water and mix it in. Continue to stir until the mixture cools.
5. Incorporate the Irish Mist and three-quarters of the cream and fold in the egg whites.
6. Spoon it into one large or several small moulds. Refrigerate and when set serve it in the moulds or unmould it and decorate it with the remaining cream.

Irish Almond Cheese Cake

250 g (8 oz) rich short crust pastry
  (see p. 141)
60 g (2 oz) butter
⅓ cup (3 oz) caster (powdered) sugar
3 eggs lightly beaten

1 cup (4 oz) chopped blanched almonds
grated rind of ½ lemon
juice of ½ lemon

1. Preheat oven to 180°C (350°F/Gas 4).
2. Roll out the pastry and line a greased flan dish.
3. Cream the butter and sugar until light and fluffy and gradually add the eggs.
4. Add the almonds, lemon rind and juice.
5. Spoon it into the flan and bake it in the preheated oven for 30 to 40 minutes or until set.

Honey Mousse

1⅓ cup (1 lb) liquid honey
4 egg yolks

4 egg whites, stiffly beaten

1. Mix the honey and egg yolks.
2. Cook in a double boiler until the mixture thickens like a custard.
3. Cool it and fold in the egg whites.
4. Pour into a glass serving bowl or individual dessert dishes and refrigerate it for 4 to 6 hours before serving.

BASIC RECIPES

Beef Stock

Meat stock is very useful in the preparation of soups and sauces; the quantity given here may seem excessive, but it can be deep frozen and kept at hand for future use.

Makes 16 cups (4 litres)

2 kg (4 lb) shin beef on the bone
2 kg (4 lb) veal knuckle (cut into 5 cm (2 in) pieces)
4 pigs trotters
2 kg (4 lb) veal and beef bones (preferably marrow bones, sawn into pieces)
60 g (2 oz) dripping

2 cups carrots, chopped
2 cups onions, chopped
1½ cups celery, chopped
1 bouquet garni of parsley, thyme, marjoram
4 bay leaves
12 black peppercorns
24 cups (6 litres) water

1. In a large saucepan, place all ingredients, except the bouquet garni, peppercorns and water and cook gently, stirring occasionally, until the meat, bones and vegetables have browned slightly.
2. Add the bouquet garni and peppercorns.
3. Add the water and slowly bring to the boil.
4. Simmer 6-8 hours until the liquid is reduced to 16 cups (4 litres).
5. Cool and strain through muslin. Skim off the fat by refrigerating the liquid overnight and removing the congealed fat the next day.

Brown Sauce

This is the basis for many other sauces and it can be refrigerated and deep-frozen for future use.

½ cup bacon, chopped
½ cup carrots, chopped
½ cup onions, chopped
½ cup celery, chopped
1 tablespoon chopped thyme
2 bay leaves

¾ cup (6 fl oz) dry white wine
1 cup (8 fl oz) brown roux
1 cup (8 fl oz) concentrated tomato purée
16 cups (4 litres) hot beef stock

1. In a large saucepan, fry the bacon, add the vegetabes and cook them gently until lightly coloured.
2. Add the thyme and bay leaves
3. Add the wine, then the roux and stir.
4. Add the tomato purée and gradually stir in the stock, making sure there are no lumps.
5. Stir frequently, while bringing the sauce to the boil, so that it does not stick to the bottom of the saucepan.
6. Place the saucepan on the flame in such a way that it is just under one edge of the saucepan.
7. Simmer 3-4 hours, stirring frequently and occasionally removing the spume which accumulates on the surface on the opposite edge to the flame.
8. The sauce should be completed when it reduces to 8 cups (2 litres) of liquid.
9. Sieve and cover the surface with plastic to prevent formation of a skin.

Brown Roux

Makes 1 cup (8 fl oz)

125 g (4 oz) butter
¾ cup (3 oz) flour

1. Melt the butter in a heavy-bottomed saucepan.
2. Take it off the heat and, stirring with a wooden spoon or whisk, add the sifted flour. Stir until the mixture is smooth.
3. Return to the heat and, stirring constantly, cook until the roux has a light brown colour.

Béchamel Sauce

White sauce

Makes 2 cups (16 fl oz)

2 cups (16 fl oz) milk
½ bay leaf
sprig of thyme
1 small onion, peeled

pinch of nutmeg
60 g (2 oz) butter
½ cup (2 oz) flour
salt and pepper

1. Bring the milk to the boil with the bay leaf, thyme, onion and nutmeg.
2. Remove the mixture from the heat and leave it to infuse for 15 minutes.
3. In a clean saucepan melt the butter, add the flour and stir well to make a roux.
4. Strain the milk into the roux, whisking well all the time until it is thick and creamy.
5. Allow to simmer gently for 3 minutes, stirring constantly, to dissipate any taste of flour.
6. Add salt and pepper to taste.

Fish Stock

Makes approximately 1¾ cups (14 fl oz)

1 kg (2 lb) fish trimmings, such as fish heads, bones, fresh or cooked shellfish leftovers
1 onion, thinly sliced
6-8 parsley stems (not the leaves; they will darken the stock)

1 teaspoon lemon juice
¼ teaspoon salt
1 cup (8 fl oz) dry white wine
cold water to cover

1. Place all the ingredients in a large heavy saucepan.
2. Bring it to the boil, skim, and simmer gently for 30 minutes.
3. Strain the stock through a fine sieve and correct the seasoning.
4. Fish stock may be refrigerated or deep frozen.

Chicken Stock

Makes 10 cups (2.5 litres)

1.5 kg (3 lb) boiling chicken with giblets
8-12 cups (2-3 litres) water
2 carrots, sliced
1 turnip, sliced
3 stalks celery, sliced

2 onions, unpeeled and halved
½ bunch parsley, roughly chopped
1 sprig thyme, chopped
6 peppercorns
3 bay leaves

1. In a large saucepan combine all the ingredients, making certain that the heart, stomach and liver have been properly cleaned.
2. Bring slowly to the boil and continue to simmer over low heat for 2-2½ hours.
3. Let all the ingredients cool in the stock, then strain, refrigerate and degrease it.
4. Discard the vegetables but keep the chicken. Remove the meat from the bones. It can be either chopped and used in a chicken soup or minced and made into chicken croquettes.
5. Use the stock in the preparation of soups and sauces. It may be refrigerated and will keep for 3-4 days or frozen when it may be kept for months.

Reform Club Sauce

To be served with lamb cutlets. This dish was devised during the Victorian era by famous French chef Alexis Soyer at the London Reform Club.

Serves 8

90 g (3 oz) thinly sliced ham or smoked tongue, finely chopped
½ cup (4 fl oz) dry sherry
1 medium onion, finely chopped
60 g (2 oz) butter
2 hard-boiled egg whites thinly sliced
90 g (3 oz) cooked beetroot, finely diced

90 g (3 oz) thinly sliced gherkins
4 cups (1 litre) brown sauce (see p. 139)
salt
freshly ground black pepper
sugar
redcurrant jelly

1. Soak the ham or tongue in sherry.
2. Sauté the onions in half of the butter until soft and transparent.
3. Add the mushrooms and sauté for 2 to 3 minutes.
4. Add the ham or tongue, the egg whites, beetroot, gherkins and the brown sauce.
5. Heat, but do not boil.
6. Gently stir in the remaining butter.
7. Season to taste with salt, pepper, sugar and redcurrant jelly. Serve in a sauceboat with Reform Club Cutlets (see p. 62).

Savoury Suet Pastry

500 g (1 lb) flour
2 tablespoons baking powder (optional)
1½ teaspoons salt

250 g (8 oz) suet, finely chopped
1¼ cups (10 fl oz) water

1. Mix all ingredients, adding enough water to make a pastry of stiff elastic consistency.

Short Crust Pastry

Makes 250 g (8 oz)

2 cups (8 oz) flour
pinch of salt
pinch of sugar

185 g (6 oz) cold butter
a little cold milk

1. Place the flour, salt, sugar and butter in a mixing bowl.
2. Rub the flour and butter together rapidly between the tips of your fingers until the butter is broken into small crumbs.
3. Add the milk and blend quickly with your hand, gathering the dough into a mass.
4. Press the dough into a roughly shaped ball — it should just hold together and be pliable, not damp and sticky.
5. Place the dough on a lightly floured pastry board and knead it gently to ensure a thorough blend of ingredients.
6. Gather it again into a ball, sprinkle it lightly with flour and wrap it in greaseproof paper.
7. Place it in the refrigerator to chill slightly before using.

INDEX
BRITAIN

IRELAND